JOHN CAL

TYRANNICAL KINGDOM

Geneva's Experiment in "Christian" Dominionism

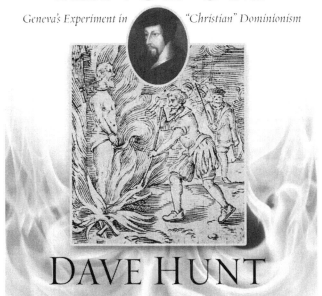

DAVE HUNT

FOREWORD BY T. A. McMAHON

BEND • OREGON

JOHN CALVIN'S TYRANNICAL KINGDOM
Geneva's "Experiment" in Christian Dominionism

by Dave Hunt

Published by The Berean Call
Copyright ©2012

ISBN 978-1-928660-76-7

Unless otherwise indicated, Scripture quotations are from
The Holy Bible, King James Version (KJV)

The Berean Call
PO Box 7019
Bend, Oregon, 97708-7020

PRINTED IN THE UNITED STATES OF AMERICA

CONTENTS

FOREWORD

*If ye then be risen with Christ, seek those things which
are above, where Christ sitteth on the right hand of
God. Set your affection on things above, not on things
on the earth. For ye are dead, and your life is hid with
Christ in God. When Christ, who is our life, shall
appear, then shall ye also appear with him in glory.*

—COLOSSIANS 3:1-4

I'M FASCINATED BY TIMELINES. They give me an idea of
what events took place in history, how they relate timewise to
other historical events, and whether or not former events may
have influenced later ones. I especially like biblical timelines.
They often begin with the event of creation and end with
the future Millennial reign of Jesus Christ from Jerusalem,
supplying a host of details in between. Due to their temporal
nature, however, they can only hint at eternity, which is infinite,
and for which our life on earth is only a preparation.

Sadly, much of the church is caught up in a temporal delusion: clinging to this earth rather than hoping for heaven. It's
part of Satan's strategy to deceive the world into building his
kingdom. For thousands of years, he has seduced both professing

and true Christians into joining his labor force, with the goal of establishing his own religion, which will be headed by his puppet ruler, the Antichrist. As the intensity of his program increases in these last days, particularly in Christendom, the leaven of this apostasy has been deposited in all theological camps: charismatics, Calvinists, conservatives, liberals, Pentecostals, Baptists, left-leaning Christians, supporters of the Emerging Church Movement, promoters of the "social gospel," et al.

In its simplest form, it is an attitude of disdaining what Paul admonishes us to do in Colossians 3:2: "Set your affection on things above, not on things on the earth." Although even those who truly know and love Jesus may struggle sometimes with keeping their affections on Him, there are others who profess Christ and claim to follow His Word yet who continue in their attempts to set up His kingdom here on earth prior to His return. That unbiblical objective, sometimes referred to as Dominion Theology and Kingdom-Dominionism, has taken many forms throughout church history.

One early example was the Holy Roman Empire. The idea was that "godly" (i.e., in support of the papacy) emperors would bring the world into the fold of Christ. When that wasn't successful, the papacy took control, ruling over most of the world at that time. As one historian describes it: "[The Church of Rome governed the medieval world and] had all the apparatus of the state: laws and law courts, taxes and tax-collectors, a great administrative machine, power of life and death over the citizens of Christendom and their enemies within and without.... Popes claimed the sole right of initiating and directing wars against unbelievers. They raised armies, conducted campaigns, and made treaties of peace in defense of their territorial interests."[1] Like most of the dogmas and practices of the Roman Catholic Church, this was contrary to what Jesus taught: "My kingdom is not of this world: if my kingdom were of this world, then would my servants fight... but now is my kingdom not from hence."

Amillennialism was the theological belief of the age, which posited that the Millennial, or 1,000-year, reign of Christ was already taking place, albeit spiritually. The worldly successes of the Roman Catholic Church seemed to support this view, but before long it succumbed to its own excesses and corruption. Although the Reformation was a reaction against the abuses of Catholicism, the Reformers kept the Catholic amillennial eschatology, along with many of its teachings and practices such as infant baptism and replacement theology (the belief that the church has replaced Israel). Verses from Scripture that spoke of blessings for Israel were spiritualized to denote the church; verses regarding Israel's punishment were ignored.

John Calvin attempted to make the city of Geneva a model of the kingdom of God, and, for his controlling effort, earned the title "the Protestant Pope." Although his goal was admirable, the results of his implementation were little different from what he had objected to in the Roman Catholic Church. Historian Will Durant writes, "The new clergy...became under Calvin more powerful than any priesthood since Israel. The real law of a Christian state, said Calvin, must be the Bible, the clergy are the interpreters of that law, civil governments are subject to that law, and must enforce it as so interpreted."[2]

Another historian writes, "In a class by themselves stood

crimes against Calvin. It was a crime to laugh at Calvin's sermons, it was a crime to argue with Calvin on the street. But to enter into a theological controversy with Calvin might turn out to be a very grave crime."[3] Geneva was hardly heaven on earth, though that was the intent. For example, "an overabundance of dishes at the table, a too-elevated headdress, an excessive display of lace, a proscribed color in dress—all were fair subjects of debate and punishment,"[4] and one never knew when the consistory (the church police) would make a house call. One year saw 400 citizens indicted for moral offenses, and, in 60 years, 150 people accused of heresy were burned at the stake.

Calvin's Christianized society was simply not biblical, substituting law for grace. Not only that, it was inconsistent with Calvinist theology. How was one to "Christianize" those in Geneva who were not among God's elect? Characterized as "totally depraved" and not able to respond righteously because they were not extended "irresistible grace," the "non-elect" could never be the Christian citizens that Calvin demanded.

Kingdom-Dominionism took on a new form in the 1940s in Saskatchewan, Canada. An alleged spiritual revival broke out that spawned the "Manifest Sons of God," or, more commonly, the Latter Rain Movement. The eschatology of this movement shifted from the dispensational view, which is the Rapture of the church followed by seven years of tribulation and ending with Armageddon. The movement promoted a more "positive," even triumphant, scenario, looking for God to pour out His Spirit in a great worldwide revival, which would produce "Manifest Sons of God," a.k.a. Joel's Army.

These would be believers, continually filled with the Spirit, who would manifest the same signs and wonders that Jesus did and would judge and conquer the world as they ushered in the 1,000-year reign of Christ.

One of the leaders of the movement has said: "God's people are going to start to exercise rule, and they're going to take dominion over the Power of Satan.... As the rod of [God's] strength goes out of Zion, He'll change legislation. He'll chase the devil off the face of God's earth, and God's people...will bring about God's purposes and God's reign."[5] This movement, however, ran into the same problems that plagued Calvin in Geneva. The so-called Manifest Sons of God couldn't live up to godly moral standards in practice, even though strict (read "abusive") measures, known as "shepherding," were applied.

The dominionism of the Latter Rain Movement spread far and wide among Pentecostals and Charismatics.... The movement was further promoted by the late Bishop Earl Paulk, who taught that Christ was "held in heaven" until His Body, the church, purified itself and the world. Paulk, however, had problems purifying himself, having had a long history of sexual immoralities and was later convicted of perjury. In the 1980s, under Paulk's leadership, charismatic Kingdom Theology joined forces with Calvinistic Dominionist Theology, also known as Christian Reconstructionism, or Theonomy.

Christian Reconstructionism was popularized by Rousas Rushdoony and his son-in-law, Gary North. Reconstructionists believe that by applying the laws of the Old Testament and the principles of the New Testament, the world will be morally transformed by Christians. This, they claimed, would draw people to Christ. Their eschatology is postmillennial, which means that they expect Christ to return after 1,000 years (viewed by some as a symbolic number, meaning that it could be much longer) of successfully reaping the fruit produced by applying the law.

From the 1980s through the turn of the century, a Reconstructionist group called the Coalition On Revival, or COR, greatly influenced conservative evangelicals to seek to transform the U.S. into a Christian-run nation by using the political process. Although the Reconstructionists and the charismatic Kingdom-Now proponents were far apart theologically, the dominionist beliefs that are basic to both camps drew them together. Gary North noted that this surprising liaison made sense in another way: "...bringing together the postmillennial Christian reconstructionists and the 'positive confession' charismatics, with the former providing the footnotes, theology, and political action skills, and the latter providing the money, the audience, and the satellite technology [e.g., TBN and Christian Broadcasting Network]."[6]

A number of years ago, a friend of mine sat in on a meeting of Reconstructionists and asked if they truly intended to apply the biblical laws such as stoning and other capital punishments, to which a national leader of the movement replied, "Absolutely!" It seems that the Calvinist Reconstructionists learned little from the failure of Calvin's totalitarian experiment in Geneva.

The Kingdom-Dominionist movement continues, especially among charismatics, to our present day (I elaborate and expand on these connections further in my book, *Temporal Delusion*). But as Dave Hunt has noted in *Whatever Happened to Heaven?* all of these movements from church history hold this in common; they are earthbound:

> The great seduction is to turn us from heaven to earth, from the true God to ourselves, from the denial of self to the acceptance, love, and esteem of oneself, from God's truth to Satan's lie. At the heart of this seduction are beliefs that have a deceptively spiritual appeal, but which actually turn us from loving Christ and His appearing to the earthly ambition of taking over society and remaking this world into the paradise that Adam and Eve lost. (p. 308)

Nearly 500 years ago, the historic seeds of protestant dominionism were sown in Geneva, Switzerland by John Calvin. These seeds have taken root 'round the world; but the fruit of Calvinism prospered greatly in the New World, and became almost inseparable from various strains of Christian nationalism that thrive on U.S. shores to this day.

We now invite the reader to consider the historic example and influence of John Calvin on the church and society of his day; and in the pages that follow, to contemplate the wisdom of perpetuating Calvin's particular theology (and peculiar methodology) for "reclaiming the culture" in our own time.

—T. A. McMahon
EXECUTIVE DIRECTOR, THE BEREAN CALL

chapter

I

CALVIN'S ROOTS—
AND INSTITUTES

THE MAN KNOWN TODAY throughout the world as John
Calvin, who is generally credited as the founder of the system
of Protestantism named after him, was born July 10, 1509, in
Noyon, France, as *Jean Chauvin*. His was a devoutly religious
Roman Catholic family of prominence in an ecclesiastical
town dominated by the local bishop and his assisting priests.
As secretary and legal advisor to the bishop, Jean's father,
Gerald, was an inside participant in a corrupt, religion-based
political system.

In a bit of old-fashioned and quite common nepo-
tism, young Jean was put on the Church payroll at the age
of twelve, remaining on it for thirteen years—until one year
after his apparent conversion to Luther's Protestantism. From

his earliest years, Jean was the beneficiary of an ungodly partnership between the civil and religious authorities, who held
the common people in bondage—a partnership dominated
by the Church. It was a pattern that he would later imple-
ment as a "Protestant" with even greater efficiency in Geneva,
Switzerland, including church dominance in civil affairs, and
persecution and even execution of those accused of heresy.

Upon entering the Collège de La Marche at the University
of Paris, Jean's love of Latin was reflected in his registration as
Johannes Calvinus. There he diligently spent excessively long
hours in compulsive study that had ill effects upon his health
in later years and possibly shortened his life. He was known for
his deep Catholic piety and blunt rebukes of his friends' morals.

Quite unexpectedly, in 1528, Jean's father, Gerald, was
excommunicated from the Roman Catholic Church. Shortly
thereafter, Calvin's brother, a priest, was also excommunicated
for heresy. As a result, Gerald ordered Jean/Johannes, who was
studying for the priesthood, to Orléans for the study of law.

Calvin later explained, "My father had intended me for
theology from my childhood. But [since] the law proved everywhere very lucrative for its practitioners, the prospect suddenly
made him change his mind."[1] This new pursuit became the
young man's passion and possibly laid some of the foundation
for the legalism that was later to become so pervasive in the
system of theology that he would thereafter develop.

After earning a Bachelor of Laws in 1531 (he would later
be granted a doctorate in law), Jean—now Johannes (John)—
returned to Paris, immersed himself in a passionate study of
classical literature, and published his first piece of writing, a
Latin essay on Seneca's *De Clementia.* Historian Will Durant

says that John, still a devout Roman Catholic, "seemed dedi-
cated to humanism, when some sermons of Luther reached
him and stirred him with their audacity."[2] Secret discussions
of daring dissension soon swept Calvin into a circle of young
humanist intellectuals who were urging reform of the Church
along the lines of Luther's bold rebellion against the Pope.

By January 1534, though not yet a full-fledged Protestant,
Calvin had become vocal enough in support of Luther's ideas
that he was forced to flee Paris. Finding refuge in the town
of Angoulême, he began to write his voluminous classic,
Institutes of the Christian Religion, and quite remarkably finished the first and smaller edition the following year. Boettner
acknowledges:

> The first [Latin] edition contained in brief outline all
> the essential elements of his system, and, considering
> the youthfulness of the author, was a marvel of intel-
> lectual precocity. It was later enlarged to five times the
> size of the original and published in French, but never
> did he make any radical departure from any of the doc-
> trines set forth in the first edition.[3]

Today's Calvinists avoid the uncomfortable fact that in all of
his voluminous writings, Calvin never tells of being born again
through faith in Christ. He considered himself to have been
a Christian from the moment of his Roman Catholic infant
baptism: "…at whatever time we are baptised, we are washed
and purified once for the whole of life…we must recall…our
baptism…so as to feel certain and secure of the remission
of sins…it wipes and washes away all our defilements."[4] He
trusted in that baptism as proof that he was one of the elect[5]

and denounced all who, like today's evangelical ex-Catholics, were baptized after believing the gospel.

Those saved out of Catholicism and baptized as believers were known as Anabaptists and were persecuted by Catholics, Lutherans, and Calvinists. Of such, near the time of his conversion to Luther's Protestantism, Calvin wrote, "One should not be content with simply killing such people, but should burn them cruelly."[6] Calvin banished them from Geneva in 1537.[7] How could today's born-again and baptized former Catholics consider Calvin as one of them? They couldn't—and wouldn't.

Calvin's Institutes

In his *Institutes*, Calvin masterfully developed his own brand of Christianity. It was without a doubt an expansion upon Augustinianism and was heavily influenced by the Latin Vulgate—the official Bible of the Roman Catholic Church and the one Calvin had long studied in its original Latin. The *Institutes*, arising from these two primary sources, has influenced succeeding generations to an extent far beyond anything its young author could have imagined at the time.

Most of those today, including evangelical leaders who hold Calvin in great esteem, are not aware that they have been captivated by the writings of a devout Roman Catholic, newly converted to Luther's Protestantism, who had broken with Rome only a year before.

Oddly, Calvin kept himself on the payroll of the Roman Catholic Church for nearly a year after he claimed to have been miraculously delivered from the "deep slough" of "obstinate addiction to the superstitions of the papacy."[8] Not until May

4, 1534, did he return to his hometown of Noyon to resign from the Bishop's employ, where he was arrested, imprisoned, managed to escape, and fled.[9] Although he was on the run and changing his place of residence, Calvin finished his original *Institutes* in August 1535. The first edition was published in March 1536.[10]

By any standard, this young man was far from mature in the Christian faith. Calvin himself said, "I was greatly astonished that, before a year passed [after he left the Roman church], all those who had some desire for pure doctrine betook themselves to me in order to learn, *although I myself had done little more than begin*" (emphasis added).[11]

Unquestionably, his *Institutes* could not possibly have come from a deep and fully developed evangelical understanding of Scripture. Instead, they came from the energetic enthusiasm of a recent law graduate and fervent student of philosophy and religion, a young zealot devoted to Augustine and a newly adopted cause. Durant says:

> [As] a lad of twenty-six, he completed the most elo-
> quent, fervent, lucid, logical, influential, and terrible
> work in all the literature of the religious revolution....
> He carried into theology and ethics the logic, precision,
> and severity of Justinian's *Institutes* and gave his own
> masterpiece a similar name.[12]

Commendably, like Luther and the other Reformers, Calvin was determined that Scripture would be his sole authority. Early in the *Institutes* he laid down that foundation, affirming that "if we look at it [the Bible] with clear eyes and unbiased judgment, it will forthwith present itself with a divine majesty which will subdue our presumptuous opposition and force us to do it homage."[13]

Calvin revered God's Word as so far surpassing anything man had ever or could ever produce that "compared with its energetic influence, the beauties of rhetoricians and philosophers will almost entirely disappear; so that it is easy to perceive something divine in the sacred Scriptures...."[14] No one can question Calvin's zeal to follow the Bible, or his sincere conviction that what he conceived and taught was true to God's Word. Nevertheless, just as the Bereans searched the Scriptures daily to determine whether Paul's teaching was true to God's Word, so we must do with Calvin's teaching.

At the time of writing his *Institutes*, Calvin, far from being an apostle like Paul, was at best a brand-new convert. Therefore, in writing the *Institutes*, Calvin sought, with his brilliant legal mind, to make up for what he lacked in spiritual maturity and guidance of the Holy Spirit. Despite his natural intelligence, however, this young zealot seemed blind to the fact that the partnership he later forged in Geneva between church and state (as Luther also did) was one of Roman Catholicism's major wrongs all over again, and the very antithesis of Christ's life and teaching. The remnants of that error still plague Europe today in the form of state churches.

Basic Elements: Sovereignty and Predestination

A basic foundation of Calvin's religious system was an extremist view of God's sovereignty that denied the human will and considered the church to be God's kingdom on earth—both views inspired by Augustine's writings. Verduin writes of Augustine, "Here we have an early representation of the notion that the Church of Christ was intended by its Founder to enter into a situation radically different from the one depicted in the New Testament.... This idea set forth by Augustine...led to all sorts of theological absurdities."[15]

Augustine taught that foreknowledge was the same as predestination: "Consequently, sometimes the same predestination is signified also under the name of foreknowledge."[16] Thus, God's foreknowledge *causes* future events. Interestingly, R. C. Sproul writes that "virtually nothing in John Calvin's view of predestination...was not first in Martin Luther, and before Luther in Augustine."[17] Calvin saw God as the author of every event, including all sin:

> If God merely foresaw human events, and did not also arrange and dispose of them at his pleasure, there might be room for agitating the question, how far his foreknowledge amounts to necessity; but since...He has decreed that they are so to happen...it is clear that all events take place by his sovereign appointment.[18]

R. C. Sproul, Jr. states plainly, "God wills all things that come to pass...God created sin."[19] Out of this extreme view of God's sovereignty came Calvin's understanding of predestination. According to him (following the teaching of Augustine), in eternity past God decided to save only a fraction of the human race and consigned the rest to eternal torment—simply because it pleased Him to do so:

> Those, therefore, whom God passes by he reprobates, and that for no other cause but because he is pleased to exclude them from the inheritance which he predestines to his children....[20]

> But if all whom the Lord predestines to death are
> naturally liable to sentence of death, of what injustice,
> pray, do they complain...because by his eternal provi-
> dence they were before their birth doomed to perpetual
> destruction...what will they be able to mutter against
> this defense?[21]
>
> Of this no other cause can be adduced than repro-
> bation, which is hidden in the secret counsel of God.[22]
> Now since the arrangement of all things is in the hand
> of God...He arranges... that individuals are born, who
> are doomed from the womb to certain death, and are to
> glorify him by their destruction....[23]
>
> God, according to the good pleasure of his will,
> without any regard to merit, elects those whom he
> chooses for sons, while he rejects and reprobates oth-
> ers.... It is right for him to show by punishing that he
> is a just judge....
>
> Here the words of Augustine most admirably
> apply.... When other vessels are made unto dishonor,
> it must be imputed not to injustice, but to judgment.[24]

In his *Institutes*, Calvin emphasizes sovereignty but scarcely
mentions God's love for sinners. Luther, too, was convinced
that God, by His own sovereign choice and independent of
anything in man, had from eternity past determined whom He
would save and whom He would damn. Calvin (like Augustine
and most Calvinists today) said God could foresee the future
only because He had willed it.[25] Here we have the horrible doctrine of reprobation from Calvin's own pen, echoing once again
his mentor, Augustine:

> We say, then that Scripture clearly proves this much,
> that God by his eternal and immutable counsel

determined once for all those whom it was his pleasure one day to admit to salvation and those whom,
on the other hand, it was his pleasure to doom to
destruction. We maintain that this counsel as regards
the elect is founded on his free mercy, without any
respect to human worth, while those whom he dooms
to destruction are excluded from access to life by a
just and blameless…incomprehensible judgment….
By excluding the reprobate…he by these marks in a
manner discloses the judgment which awaits them.[26]

Depravity and "Mystery"

God's mercy as Calvin understood it was very limited. He
majors upon God's justice; unquestionably, God would be just
in damning the entire human race. The real question, however,
is whether God who *is love* would neglect to make salvation
available to *anyone*—much less predestine to damnation
multitudes whom He *could* save if He so desired. The Bible
clearly declares God's love for all mankind and His desire that
all should be saved. It is in defense of God's love and character
that we propose to test Calvinism against God's Word.

According to Calvin, rather than salvation depending upon
whether a person freely believed the gospel, it depended upon
whether God had predestined him to salvation. No one could
believe unto salvation without God regenerating and then producing in those whom He had chosen the faith to believe. This
conclusion followed logically from Calvin's extreme view of
human depravity, which he laid out in his first writings:

> The mind of man is so completely alienated from the
> righteousness of God that it conceives, desires, and
> undertakes everything that is impious, perverse, base,
> impure, and flagitious. His heart is so thoroughly
> infected by the poison of sin that it cannot produce
> anything but what is corrupt; and if at any time men
> do anything apparently good, yet the mind always
> remains involved in hypocrisy and deceit, and the heart
> enslaved by its inward perversity.[27]

By *Total Depravity*, Calvinism means total *inability*. Left
to themselves, all men not only do not seek God but are *totally
unable* to seek Him, much less to believe in Jesus Christ to the
saving of their souls. As a consequence of this total inability,
God *causes some* to believe just as He causes *all* to sin.

We must then conclude that God, who *is love*, doesn't love
all men enough to rescue them from eternal punishment but
reserves His love for a select group called the elect.

Some Calvinists attempt to deny that Calvin taught that
God decreed the damnation of the lost from whom He with-
held the Irresistible Grace that He bestowed upon the elect.
Instead, they say that He simply "leaves the non-elect in his just
judgment to their own wickedness and obduracy."[28]

Like Augustine, however, Calvin says it both ways. Clearly,
to *allow* anyone whom God *could* rescue to go to hell (no matter how much they deserved it) is the same as *consigning* them
to that fate, which Calvin called "reprobation." Nor is there
any question that, through Calvinism's Irresistible Grace, God
could save the entire human race if He desired to do so. Surely,
Infinite Love would not allow those loved to suffer eternal torment—yet God, according to Calvinism, is pleased to damn

billions. Such teaching misrepresents the God of the Bible, as we shall document from Scripture.

In the final analysis, no rationalization can explain away the bluntness of Calvin's language—that some were by God's "pleasure [in] his eternal providence...before their birth doomed to perpetual destruction...." This sovereign consigning of some to bliss and others to torment was a display of God's power that would, according to Calvin, "promote our admiration of His glory."[29]

Even non-Christians find it a shocking doctrine that God is glorified in predestinating some to salvation and others to damnation, though there is no difference in merit between the saved and lost. That God would leave *anyone* to eternal torment who could be rescued, however, would demean God, since to do so is repugnant to the conscience and compassion that God has placed within all mankind!

Calvin himself admitted that this doctrine was repulsive to intelligent reason. As in Roman Catholicism, Calvin sought to escape the obvious contradictions in his system by pleading "mystery":

> Paul...rising to the sublime mystery of predestination....[30]
>
> How sinful it is to insist on knowing the causes of the divine will, since it is itself, and justly ought to be, the cause of all that exists.... Therefore, when it is asked why the Lord did so, we must answer, because he pleased.... Of this no other cause can be adduced than reprobation, which is hidden in the secret counsel of God.[31]

Calvin claims to derive from the Bible the teaching that God, to His glory, predestined vast multitudes to eternal damnation without allowing them any choice. In fact, while he was still a Roman Catholic he had doubtless already come to such a conclusion from his immersion in the writings of Augustine and the official (and badly corrupted) Roman Catholic Bible, the Latin Vulgate.

C.H. Spurgeon, though a Calvinist (whom Calvinists love to quote in their support) who at times confirmed Limited Atonement, was unable to escape his God-given conscience. His evangelist's heart often betrayed itself in statements expressing a compassion for the lost and a desire for their salvation—a compassion that contradicted the Calvinism he preached at other times. For example:

> As it is *my* wish [and] *your* wish…so it is God's wish that all men should be saved…he is no less benevolent than we are.[32]

It is impossible to reconcile that statement with the doctrine of Limited Atonement, which Spurgeon at other times affirmed. It is irrational to say that God sincerely desires the salvation of all, yet sent His Son to die for only some. But this, as we shall see, is just one of many contradictions in which Calvinism traps its adherents.

chapter

2

CALVINISM'S SURPRISING CATHOLIC CONNECTION

THERE IS NO QUESTION that Calvin imposed upon the Bible certain erroneous interpretations from his Roman Catholic background. Many leading Calvinists agree that the writings of Augustine were the actual source of most of what is known as Calvinism today. Calvinists David Steele and Curtis Thomas point out that "The basic doctrines of the Calvinistic position had been vigorously defended by Augustine against Pelagius during the fifth century."[1]

In his eye-opening book, *The Other Side of Calvinism*, Laurence M. Vance thoroughly documents that "John Calvin did not originate the doctrines that bear his name...."[2] Vance quotes numerous well-known Calvinists to this effect. For example, Kenneth G. Talbot and W. Gary Crampton write,

"The system of doctrine which bears the name of John Calvin was in no way originated by him...."[3] B. B. Warfield declared, "The system of doctrine taught by Calvin is just the Augustinianism common to the whole body of the Reformers."[4] Thus the debt that the creeds coming out of the Reformation owe to Augustine is also acknowledged. This is not surprising in view of the fact that most of the Reformers had been part of the Roman Catholic Church, of which Augustine was one of the most highly regarded "saints." John Piper acknowledges that Augustine was the major influence upon both Calvin and Luther, who continued to revere him and his doctrines even after they broke away from Roman Catholicism.[5]

C. H. Spurgeon admitted that "perhaps Calvin himself derived it [Calvinism] mainly from the writings of Augustine."[6] Alvin L. Baker wrote, "There is hardly a doctrine of Calvin that does not bear the marks of Augustine's influence."[7] For example, the following from Augustine sounds like an echo reverberating through the writings of Calvin:

> Even as he has appointed them to be regenerated... whom he predestinated to everlasting life, as the most merciful bestower of grace, whilst to those whom he has predestinated to eternal death, he is also the most righteous awarder of punishment.[8]

C. Gregg Singer said, "The main features of Calvin's theology are found in the writings of St. Augustine to such an extent that many theologians regard Calvinism as a more fully developed form of Augustinianism."[9] Such statements are staggering declarations in view of the undisputed fact that, as Vance points out, the Roman Catholic Church itself has a better claim on

Augustine than do the Calvinists.[10] Calvin himself said:

> Augustine is so wholly with me, that if I wished to write
> a confession of my faith, I could do so with all fulness
> and satisfaction to myself out of his writings.[11]

Augustine and the Use of Force

The fourth century Donatists believed that the church should be
a pure communion of true believers who demonstrated the truth
of the gospel in their lives. They abhorred the apostasy that had
come into the church when Constantine wedded Christianity
to paganism in order to unify the empire. Compromising clergy
were "evil priests working hand in glove with the kings of the
earth, who show that they have no king but Caesar." To the
Donatists, the church was a "small body of saved surrounded
by the unregenerate mass."[12] This is, of course, the biblical view.

Augustine, on the other hand, saw the church of his day
as a mixture of believers and unbelievers, in which purity and
evil should be allowed to exist side by side for the sake of unity.
He used the power of the state to compel church attendance
(as Calvin also would 1,200 years later): "Whoever was not
found within the Church was not asked the reason, but was to
be corrected and converted...."[13] Calvin followed his mentor
Augustine in enforcing church attendance and participation
in the sacraments by threats (and worse) against the citizens
of Geneva. Augustine "identified the Donatists as heretics...
who could be subjected to imperial legislation [and force]
in exactly the same way as other criminals and misbelievers,
including poisoners and pagans."[14] Frend says of Augustine,

"The questing, sensitive youth had become the father of the inquisition."[15]

Though he preferred persuasion if possible, Augustine supported military force against those who were rebaptized as believers after conversion to Christ and for other alleged heretics. In his controversy with the Donatists, using a distorted and un-Christian interpretation of Luke 14:23,[16] Augustine declared:

> Why therefore should not the Church use force in compelling her lost sons to return?... The Lord Himself said, "Go out into the highways and hedges and compel them to come in...." Wherefore is the power which the Church has received...through the religious character and faith of kings...the instrument by which those who are found in the highways and hedges—that is, in heresies and schisms—are compelled to come in, and let them not find fault with being compelled.[17]

Sadly, Calvin put into effect in Geneva the very principles of punishment, coercion, and death that Augustine advocated and that the Roman Catholic Church followed consistently for centuries. Henry H. Milman writes: "Augustinianism was worked up into a still more rigid and uncompromising system by the severe intellect of Calvin."[18] And he justified himself by Augustine's erroneous interpretation of Luke 14:23. How could any who today hail Calvin as a great exegete accept such abuse of this passage?

Compel? Isn't that God's job through Unconditional Election and Irresistible Grace? *Compel* those for whom Christ didn't die and whom God has predestined to eternal torment? This verse refutes Calvinism no matter how it is intepreted!

Augustine's Dominant Influence

There is no question as to the important role Augustine played in molding Calvin's thinking, theology, and actions. This is particularly true concerning the key foundations of Calvinism. Warfield refers to Calvin and Augustine as "two extraordinarily gifted men [who] tower like pyramids over the scene of history."[19] Calvin's *Institutes of the Christian Religion* make repeated favorable references to Augustine, frequently citing his writings as authoritative and using the expression, "Confirmed by the authority of Augustine."[20] Calvin often credits Augustine with having formulated key concepts, which he then expounds in his *Institutes*. The following are but a very small sampling of such references:

- "We have come into the way of faith," says Augustine: "Let us constantly adhere to it...."[21]

- The truth of God is too powerful, both here and everywhere, to dread the slanders of the ungodly, as Augustine powerfully maintains.... Augustine disguises not that...he was often charged with preaching the doctrine of predestination too freely, but...he abundantly refutes the charge.... For it has been shrewdly observed by Augustine (De Genesi ad litteram, Lib V) that we can safely follow Scripture....[22]

- For Augustine, rightly expounding this passage, says....[23]

- I say with Augustine, that the Lord has created those who, as he certainly foreknew, were to go to destruction, and he did so because he so willed.[24]

- If your mind is troubled, decline not to embrace the counsel of Augustine....[25]

- I will not hesitate, therefore, simply to confess with Augustine that...those things will certainly happen which he [God] has foreseen [and] that the destruction [of the non-elect] consequent upon predestination is also most just.[26]

- Augustine, in two passages in particular, gives a [favorable] portraiture of the form of ancient monasticism. [Calvin then proceeds to quote Augustine's commendation of the early monks.][27]

- Here the words of Augustine most admirably apply....[28]

- This is a faithful saying from Augustine; but because his words will perhaps have more authority than mine, let us adduce the following passage from his treatise....[29]

- Wherefore, Augustine not undeservedly orders such, as senseless teachers or sinister and ill-omened prophets, to retire from the Church.[30]

We could multiply many times over the above examples of Augustine's influence upon Calvin from the scores of times Calvin quotes extensively from Augustine's writings. Leading Calvinists admit that Calvin's basic beliefs were already formed while he was still a devout Roman Catholic, through the writings of Augustine—an influence that remained with him throughout his life.

Augustinian teachings that Calvin presented in his *Institutes* included the sovereignty that made God the cause of all (including sin), the predestination of some to salvation and of others to damnation, election and reprobation, faith as an irresistible gift from God—in fact, the key concepts at the heart of Calvinism.

We search in vain for evidence that Calvin ever disapproved

of any of Augustine's heresies. Calvinist Richard A. Muller admits, "John Calvin was part of a long line of thinkers who based their doctrine of predestination on the Augustinian interpretation of St. Paul."[31] In each expanded edition of his *Institutes*, Calvin quotes and relies upon Augustine more than ever.

Is Calvinism Really a Protestant Belief?

That many prominent evangelicals today are still under the spell of Augustine is evident—and astonishing, considering his numerous heresies. Norm Geisler has said, "St. Augustine was one of the greatest Christian thinkers of all time."[32] Yet Augustine said, "I should not believe the gospel unless I were moved to do so by the authority of the [Catholic] Church."[33] That statement was quoted with great satisfaction by Pope John Paul II in his 1986 celebration of the 1600th anniversary of Augustine's conversion. The Pope went on to say:

> Augustine's legacy...is the theological methods to which he remained absolutely faithful...full adherence to the authority of the faith...revealed through Scripture, Tradition and the Church.... Likewise the profound sense of mystery—"for it is better," he exclaims, "to have a faithful ignorance than a presumptuous knowledge...." I express once again my fervent desire...that the authoritative teaching of such a great doctor and pastor may flourish ever more happily in the Church....[34]

In my debate with him, James White claims that "Calvin refuted this very passage in *Institutes*, and any fair reading of Augustine's own writings disproves this misrepresentation by

Hunt."[35] In fact, Calvin acknowledged the authenticity of the statement and attempted to defend it as legitimate reasoning for those who had not the assurance of faith by the Holy Spirit.[36]

Vance provides numerous astonishing quotations from Calvinists praising Augustine: "One of the greatest theological and philosophical minds that God has ever so seen fit to give to His church."[37] "The greatest Christian since New Testament times...greatest man that ever wrote Latin."[38] "[His] labors and writings, more than those of any other man in the age in which he lived, contributed to the promotion of sound doctrine and the revival of true religion."[39]

Warfield adds, "Augustine determined for all time the doctrine of grace."[40] Yet he [Augustine] believed that grace came through the Roman Catholic sacraments. That Calvinists shower such praise upon Augustine makes it easier to comprehend why they heap the same praise on Calvin.

As for the formation of Roman Catholicism's doctrines and practices, Augustine's influence was the greatest in history. Vance reminds us that Augustine was "one of Catholicism's original four 'Doctors of the Church' [with] a feast day [dedicated to him] in the Catholic Church on August 28, the day of his death."[41] Pope John Paul II has called Augustine "the common father of our Christian civilization."[42] William P. Grady, on the other hand, writes, "The deluded Augustine (354–430) went so far as to announce (through his book, *The City of God*) that Rome had been privileged to usher in the millennial kingdom (otherwise known as the 'Dark Ages')."[43]

Drawing from a Polluted Stream

Sir Robert Anderson reminds us that "the Roman [Catholic] Church was molded by Augustine into the form it has ever since maintained. Of all the errors that later centuries developed in the teachings of the church, scarcely one cannot be found in embryo in his writings."[44] Those errors include infant baptism for regeneration (infants who die unbaptized are damned), the necessity of baptism for the remission of sins (martyrdom, as in Islam, does the same), purgatory, salvation in the Church alone through its sacraments, and persecution of those who reject Catholic dogmas. Augustine also fathered acceptance of the Apocrypha (which he admitted even the Jews rejected), allegorical interpretation of the Bible (thus the creation account, the six days, and other details in Genesis are not necessarily literal), and rejection of the literal personal reign of Christ on earth for a thousand years (we are now supposedly in the millennial reign of Christ with the Church reigning and the devil presently bound).

Augustine insists that Satan is now "bound" on the basis that "even now men are, and doubtless to the end of the world shall be, converted to the faith from the unbelief in which he [Satan] held them." That he views the promised binding of Satan in the "bottomless pit" (Revelation 20:1–3) allegorically is clear. Amazingly, Satan "is bound in each instance in which he is spoiled of one of his goods [i.e., someone believes in Christ]." And even more amazing, "the abyss in which he is shut up" is somehow construed by Augustine to be "in the depths" of Christ-rejecters' "blind hearts." It is thus that Satan is continually shut up as in an abyss.[45]

Augustine doesn't attempt to explain how he arrived at such an astonishing idea, much less how one abyss could exist in millions of hearts or how, being "bound" there, Satan would still be free to blind those within whose "hearts" he is supposedly bound (2 Corinthians 4:4). Nor does he explain how or why, in spite of Satan's being bound,

- Christ commissioned Paul to turn Jew and Gentile "from the power of Satan unto God" (Acts 26:18)

- Paul could deliver the Corinthian fornicator to Satan (1 Corinthians 5:5)

- Satan can transform himself "into an angel of light" (2 Corinthians 11:14)

- Paul would warn the Ephesian believers not to "give place to the devil" (Ephesians 4:27) and urge them and us today to "stand against the wiles of the devil" (6:11)

- Satan could still be going about "like a roaring lion... seeking whom he may devour" (1 Peter 5:8)

- Satan could still be able to continually accuse Christians before God and, with his angels, yet wage war in heaven against "Michael and his angels" and at last be cast out of heaven to earth (Revelation 12:7–10)

Augustine was one of the first to place the authority of tradition on a level with the Bible, and to incorporate much philosophy, especially Platonism, into his theology. Exposing the folly of those who praise Augustine, Vance writes:

> He believed in apostolic succession from Peter as one
> of the marks of the true church, taught that Mary was
> sinless and promoted her worship. He was the first
> who defined the so-called sacraments as a visible sign
> of invisible grace.... The memorial of the Lord's supper
> became that of the spiritual presence of Christ's body
> and blood. To Augustine the only true church was the
> Catholic Church. Writing against the Donatists, he
> asserted: "The Catholic Church alone is the body of
> Christ.... Outside this body the Holy Spirit giveth life
> to no one...[and] he is not a partaker of divine love who
> is the enemy of unity. Therefore they have not the Holy
> Ghost who are outside the Church."[46]

And this is the man whom Geisler calls "one of the greatest
Christian thinkers of all time." On the contrary, Calvin drew
from a badly polluted stream when he embraced the teachings of
Augustine! How could one dip into such contaminating heresy
without becoming confused and infected? Yet this bewildering
muddle of speculation and formative Roman Catholicism is
acknowledged to be the source of Calvinism—and is praised
by leading evangelicals. One comes away dumbfounded at the
acclaim heaped upon both Calvin and Augustine by otherwise
sound Christian leaders.

An Amazing Contradiction

Calvin's almost complete agreement with and repeated praise
of Augustine cannot be denied. Calvin called himself "an
Augustinian theologian."[47] Of Augustine he said, "whom we
quote frequently, as being the best and most faithful witness of
all antiquity."[48]

Calvinists themselves insist upon the connection between Calvin and Augustine. McGrath writes, "Above all, Calvin regarded his thought as a faithful exposition of the leading ideas of Augustine of Hippo."[49] Wendel concedes, "Upon points of doctrine he borrows from St. Augustine with both hands."[50] Vance writes:

> Howbeit, to prove conclusively that Calvin was a disciple of Augustine, we need look no further than Calvin himself. One can't read five pages in Calvin's *Institutes* without seeing the name of Augustine. Calvin quotes Augustine over four hundred times in the *Institutes* alone. He called Augustine by such titles as "holy man" and "holy father."[51]

As Vance further points out, "Calvinists admit that Calvin was heavily influenced by Augustine in forming his doctrine of predestination."[52] How could one of the leaders of the Reformation embrace so fully the doctrines of one who has been called the "principal theological creator of the Latin-Catholic system as distinct from…Evangelical Protestantism…"?[53]

Calvin's admiration of Augustine and his embracing of much of his teaching is only one of several major contradictions in his life, which will be fully documented in this book. The situation is contradictory on the Roman Catholic side as well. Their dogmas reject some of the most important doctrines held by the most famous of their saints—the very Augustinian doctrines that Calvin embraced.

Here we confront a strange anomaly. Warfield declares that "it is Augustine who gave us the Reformation"[54]—yet at the same time, he also acknowledges that Augustine was "in a true sense the founder of Roman Catholicism"[55] and "the creator of the Holy Roman Empire."[56]

Strangely, Calvin apparently failed to recognize that Augustine never understood salvation by grace alone through faith alone in Christ alone. Philip F. Congdon writes, "Another curious parallel is evident between Classical Calvinist theology and Roman Catholic theology. The two share an inclusion of works in the gospel message, and an impossibility of assurance of salvation.... Both hold to the primacy of God's grace; both include the necessity of our works."[57] Augustine's heresies, especially his Romanist view of faith in Christ being supplemented by good works and the sacraments, were not lost on Luther, who wrote: "In the beginning, I devoured Augustine, but when...I knew what justification by faith really was, then it was out with him."[58]

Yet leading Calvinists suggest that I side with Roman Catholicism by rejecting Calvinism, even though it comes largely from the ultimate Roman Catholic, Augustine. Here is how one writer expressed it to me:

> And given that the position you espouse is, in fact, utterly opposed to the very heart of the message of the Reformers, and is instead in line with Rome's view of man's will and the nature of grace, I find it *tremendously* inconsistent on your part. You speak often of opposing the traditions of men, yet, in this case, you embrace the very traditions that lie at the heart of Rome's "gospel."[59]

On the contrary, the Reformers and their creeds are infected with ideas that came from the greatest Roman Catholic, Augustine himself. Furthermore, a rejection of

Election, Predestination, and the Preservation of the Saints as defined by Calvinists is hardly embracing "the heart of Rome's 'gospel.'" The real heart of Rome's gospel is good works and sacraments. Certainly Calvin's retention of sacramentalism, baptismal regeneration for infants, and honoring the Roman Catholic priesthood as valid is a more serious embrace of Catholicism's false gospel. The rejection of Calvinism requires no agreement with Rome whatsoever on any part of its heretical doctrines of salvation.

It seems incomprehensible that the predominant influence upon Reformed theology and creeds could be so closely related to the very Roman Catholicism against which the Reformers rebelled. Yet those who fail to bow to these creeds are allegedly "in error." How the Protestant creeds came to be dominated by Calvinistic doctrine is an interesting story.

The Role of the Latin Vulgate

Along with the writings of Augustine, the Latin Vulgate also molded Calvin's thoughts as expressed in his *Institutes of the Christian Religion*. Fluent in Latin, Calvin had long used that corrupted translation of the Bible, which, since its composition by Jerome at the beginning of the fifth century, was the official Bible of Roman Catholics. It was again so declared by the Council of Trent in 1546, when Calvin was 37 years of age. More than that, its influence reached into the Protestant movement: "For one thousand years the Vulgate was practically the only Bible known and read in Western Europe. All commentaries were based upon the Vulgate text.... Preachers based their sermons on it."[60]

The Vulgate was permeated with Augustinian views on predestination and the rejection of free will. According to Philip

Schaff, "The Vulgate can be charged, indeed, with innumerable faults, inaccuracies, inconsistencies, and arbitrary dealing in particulars."[61] Others have expressed the same opinion. Samuel Fisk quotes Samuel Berger, who in the *Cambridge History of the English Bible*, Vol. 3 (S. L. Greenslade, ed., Cambridge, England: University Press, 1963, 414), called the Vulgate "the most vulgarized and bastardized text imaginable."[62] Grady says, "Damasus commissioned Jerome to revive the archaic Old Latin Bible in A.D. 382...the completed monstrosity became known as the Latin 'Vulgate'...and was used of the devil to usher in the Dark Ages."[63] Fisk reminds us:

> Well-known examples of far-reaching errors include the whole system of Catholic "penance," drawn from the Vulgate's "do penance"...when the Latin should have followed the Greek—*repent*.
>
> Likewise the word "sacrament" was a mis-reading from the Vulgate of the original word for *mystery*. Even more significant, perhaps, was the rendering of the word *presbyter* (elder) as "priest."[64]

Augustine described the problem that led to the production of the Vulgate: "In the earliest days of the faith, when a Greek manuscript came into anyone's hands, and he thought he possessed a little facility in both languages, he ventured to make a translation [into Latin]."[65] As a consequence of such individual endeavor, Bruce says, "The time came, however, when the multiplicity of [Latin] texts [of Scripture] became too inconvenient to be tolerated any longer, and Pope Damasus... commissioned his secretary, Jerome, to undertake the work" of revision to produce one authorized Latin version.

Bruce continues: "He [Jerome] was told to be cautious for the sake of 'weaker brethren' who did not like to see their favorite texts tampered with, even in the interests of greater accuracy. Even so, he went much too far for the taste of many, while he himself knew that he was not going far enough."[66] *Unger's Bible Dictionary* comments:

> For many centuries it [Vulgate] was the only Bible generally used.... In the age of the Reformation the Vulgate [influenced] popular versions. That of Luther (N. T. in 1523) was the most important and in this the Vulgate had great weight. From Luther the influence of the Latin passed to our own Authorized Version [KJV]....[67]

The Geneva and King James Bibles and Protestant Creeds

Of no small importance to our study is the fact that this corrupt translation had an influence upon the Protestant churches in Europe, England, and America. That influence carried over into the Geneva Bible (which has further problems; see below) as well as into other early versions of the English Bible, and even into the King James Bible of today.

As the Vulgate was filled with Augustinianisms, the Geneva Bible was filled with Calvinism, in the text as well as in voluminous notes. H. S. Miller's *General Biblical Introduction* says, "It was a revision of Tyndale's, with an Introduction by Calvin... the work of English reformers, assisted by Beza, Calvin, and possibly others." J. R. Dore, in *Old Bibles: An Account of the Early Versions of the English Bible*, 2nd edition, adds that "almost every chapter [of the Geneva Bible] has voluminous notes full of Calvinistic doctrine." Andrew Edgar, in *The Bibles of England*, declares, "At the time the Geneva Bible was first published, Calvin was the ruling spirit in Geneva. All the features of his theological, ecclesiastical, political, and social system are accordingly reflected in the marginal annotations.... The doctrine of predestination is proclaimed to be the head cornerstone of the gospel."[68]

W. Hoare says in *The Evolution of the English Bible*, "Considered as a literary whole it [the Geneva Bible] has about it the character of a Calvinist manifesto...a book with a special purpose." F. F. Bruce adds,

> The notes of the Geneva Bible...are, to be sure, unashamedly Calvinistic in doctrine.... The people of England and Scotland...learned much of their biblical exegesis from these notes.... The Geneva Bible immediately won, and retained, widespread popularity. It became the household Bible of English-speaking Protestants.... This became the authorized Bible in Scotland and was brought to America where it had a strong influence.[69]

Butterworth points out: "In the lineage of the King James Bible this [Geneva Bible] is by all means the most important single volume.... The Geneva Bible...had a very great influence in the shaping of the King James Bible."[70] Robinson is even more emphatic:

> A large part of its [Geneva Bible] innovations are included in the Authorized Version [KJV].... Sometimes the Geneva text and the Geneva margin are taken over intact, sometimes the text becomes the margin and

> the margin the text. Sometimes the margin becomes
> the text and no alternative is offered. Very often the
> Genevan margin becomes the Authorized Version text
> with or without verbal change.[71]

Further documentation could be given, but this should
be sufficient to trace briefly the influence from that ultimate
Roman Catholic, Augustine, through the Latin Vulgate and his
writings, upon Calvin—and through Calvin, into the Geneva
Bible and on into the King James Bible. And thus into the pulpits and homes of Protestants throughout Europe, England,
and America. It is small wonder, then, that those who, like
Arminius, dared to question Calvinism, were overwhelmed with
opposition. Of course, various synods and assemblies were held
to formulate accepted creeds and to punish the dissenters, but
the decks were stacked in favor of Calvinism, and no influence
to mitigate this error was allowed. This will be documented in
the next chapter. [For additional detail, see *T.U.L.I.P. and the
Bible: Comparing the Works of Calvin to the Word of God,* and
What Love Is This? Calvinism's Misrepresentation of God.]

The New Geneva Study Bible *and Reformation Truth*

Today's *New Geneva Study Bible* (recently reprinted as *The
Reformation Study Bible*) is being widely distributed in an effort
to indoctrinate the readers into Calvinism. Its New King James
translation is appealing. As with the original Geneva Bible,
however, the notes are Calvinistic treatises. In his foreword,
R. C. Sproul writes,

> The *New Geneva Study Bible* is so called because it stands
> in the tradition of the original Geneva Bible.... The
> light of the Reformation was the light of the Bible....
> The Geneva Bible was published in 1560...[and] domi-
> nated the English-speaking world for a hundred years....
> Pilgrims and Puritans carried the Geneva Bible to the
> shores of the New World. American colonists were
> reared on the Geneva Bible.... The New Geneva Study
> Bible contains a modern restatement of Reformation
> truth in its comments and theological notes. Its pur-
> pose is to present the light of the Reformation afresh.

In fact, its purpose is to indoctrinate the reader into
Calvinism, which inaccurately is marketed as "Reformation
truth"—as though Calvinism and Protestantism are identi-
cal. There was, in fact, much more to the Reformation than
Calvinism, Calvinists' claims notwithstanding.

The Necessity to Clarify Confusion

Calvinism is experiencing resurgence today. Yet there is
widespread ignorance of what both Augustine and Calvin
really taught and practiced. Has the truth been suppressed to
further a particular theology? Consider Boettner's declaration
that "Calvin and Augustine easily rank as the two outstanding
systematic expounders of the Christian system since Saint
Paul."[72] Spurgeon, also declared: "Augustine obtained his views,
without doubt, through the Spirit of God, from the diligent
study of the writings of Paul, and Paul received them of the
Holy Ghost, from Jesus Christ".[73]

One cannot but view such statements with astonishment. How incredible that Loraine Boettner, one of the foremost apologists opposing the Roman Catholic Church, praised Augustine, who gave the Roman Catholic Church so many of its basic doctrines that he is among the most highly honored of its "saints" to this day.

As for Spurgeon, would he have considered that Augustine's teaching of salvation by the Roman Catholic Church, through its sacraments alone, beginning with regeneration by infant baptism; the use of force even to the death against "heretics"; acceptance of the Apocrypha; allegorical interpretation of creation and the prophecies concerning Israel; a rejection of the literal reign of Christ on David's throne; and so much other false doctrine, had also all been received from the Holy Spirit? How could Augustine—and Calvin, who embraced and passed on many of his major errors—be so wrong on so much and yet be biblically sound as regards predestination, election, sovereignty, etc.? Is there not ample cause to examine carefully these foundational teachings of Calvinism?

One can only respond in the affirmative. For that reason, the key Calvinist doctrines will be presented in the following pages and compared carefully with God's Word.

chapter

3

IRRESISTIBLY IMPOSED "CHRISTIANITY"

ONE OF SATAN'S CLEVEREST and most effective strategies was to delude the Emperor Constantine with a false conversion. The influence of that one event upon subsequent history, both religious and secular, is incalculable. Accounts differ, but whether this came about through a vision or a dream as recounted by Eusebius and Lactantius,[1] Constantine saw a "cross" in the sky and heard a "voice" proclaiming (by some accounts the words were inscribed on the cross), "In this sign thou shalt conquer." In the prior year, the god Apollo had also promised him victory.

Constantine's edicts of toleration gave every man "a right to choose his religion according to the dictates of his own conscience and honest conviction, without compulsion and interference from the government."[2] Schaff views Constantine's conversion as a wonderful advance for Christianity: "The church ascends the throne of the Caesars under the banner of the cross, and gives new vigor and lustre to the hoary empire of Rome."[3] In fact, that "conversion" accelerated the corruption of the church through its marriage to the world.[4]

How could a true follower of the Christ, whose kingdom is not of this world and whose servants do not wage war, proceed to wage war in His name? How could a true follower, under the banner of His cross, proceed to conquer with the sword? Of course, the Crusaders later did the same, slaughtering both Muslims and Jews to retake the "holy land" under Pope Urban II's pledge (matching Muhammad's and the Qur'an's promise to Muslims) of full forgiveness of sins for those who died in this holy war (Muslims call it *jihad*). The Crusades, of course, like all of the popes' wars, were very Augustinian. The City of God had to be defended!

From Constantine to Augustine

As Durant and other historians have pointed out, Constantine never renounced his loyalty to the pagan gods. He abolished neither the Altar of Victory in the Senate nor the Vestal Virgins who tended the sacred fire of the goddess Vesta. The Sun-god, not Christ, continued to be honored on the imperial coins. In spite of the "cross" (actually the cross of the god Mithras) on his shields and military banners, Constantine had a medallion created honoring the Sun for the "liberation" of Rome; and when he prescribed a day of rest, it was again in the name of the Sun-god ("the day celebrated by the veneration of the Sun"[5]) and not the Son of God.[6] Durant reminds us that throughout his "Christian" life, Constantine used pagan as well as Christian rites and continued to rely upon "pagan magic formulas to protect crops and heal disease."[7]

That Constantine murdered those who might have had a claim to his throne, including his son Crispus, a nephew, and brother-in-law, is further indication that his "conversion" was, as many historians agree, a clever political maneuver to unite the empire. Historian Philip Hughes, himself a Catholic priest, reminds us, "in his manners he [Constantine] remained, to the end, very much the Pagan of his early life. His furious tempers, the cruelty which, once aroused, spared not the lives even of his wife and son, are...an unpleasing witness to the imperfection of his conversion."[8]

It was not long after the new tolerance that Constantine found himself faced with a problem he had never anticipated: division within the Christian church to which he had given freedom. As we noted in the last chapter, it came to a head in North Africa with the Donatists, who, concerned for purity of the faith, separated from the official state churches, rejected their ordinances, and insisted on rebaptizing clergy who had repented after having denied the faith during the persecutions that arose when the Emperor Diocletian demanded that he be worshiped as a god.[9] After years of futile efforts to reestablish unity through discussion, pleadings, councils, and decrees, Constantine finally resorted to force. Frend explains:

> In the spring of 317 he [Constantine] followed up his decision by publishing a "most severe" edict against the Donatists, confiscating their property and exiling their leaders. Within four years the universal freedom

of conscience proclaimed at Milan had been abro-
gated, and the state had become a persecutor once
more, only this time in favor of Christian orthodoxy....
[The Donatists] neither understood nor cared about
Constantine's conversion. For them it was a case of
the Devil insisting that "Christ was a lover of unity"....
In their view, the fundamental hostility of the state
toward the [true] church had not been altered.[10]

In his own day and way, Augustine followed Constantine's
lead in his treatment of the Donatists, who were still a thorn
in the side of the Roman Church. "While Augustine and the
Catholics emphasized the unity of the Church, the Donatists
insisted upon the purity of the Church and rebaptized all
those who came to them from the Catholics—considering
the Catholics corrupt."[11] Constantine had been "relentless [as
would be Augustine and his disciple Calvin] in his pursuit of
'heretics' [forbidding] those outside of the Catholic church to
assemble...and confiscated their property.... The very things
Christians had endured themselves were now being practiced in
the name of Christianity."[12]

As a good citizen enjoying the blessing of the Emperor,
and believing in the state church Constantine had established,
Augustine persecuted and even sanctioned the killing of the
Donatists and other schismatics, as we have already seen. Gibbon
tells us that the severe measures against the Donatists "obtained
the warmest approbation of St. Augustine [and thereby] great
numbers of the Donatists were reconciled to [forced back into]
the Catholic Church."[13]

Of Augustine it has been said that "the very greatness
of his name has been the means of perpetuating the grossest

errors which he himself propagated. More than anyone else, Augustine has encouraged the pernicious doctrine of salvation through the sacraments of an organized earthly Church, which brought with it priestcraft with all the evil and miseries that has entailed down through the centuries."[14]

From Augustine to Calvin

There is no question that John Calvin still viewed the church of Christ through Roman Catholic eyes. He saw the church (as Constantine had molded it and Augustine had cemented it) as a partner of the state, with the state enforcing orthodoxy (as the state church defined it) upon all its citizens. Calvin applied his legal training and zeal to the development of a *system* of Christianity based upon an extreme view of God's sovereignty, which, by the sheer force of its logic, would compel kings and all mankind to conform all affairs to righteousness. In partnership with the church, kings and other civil rulers would enforce Calvinistic Christianity.

Of those who believed in a thousand-year reign of Christ upon earth, Calvin said their "fiction is too puerile to need or to deserve refutation."[15] As far as Calvin was concerned, Christ's kingdom began with His advent upon earth and had been in process ever since. Rejecting the literal future reign of Christ upon the earth through His Second Coming to establish an earthly kingdom upon David's throne in Jerusalem, Calvin apparently felt obliged to establish the kingdom by his own efforts in Christ's absence.

The Bible makes it clear that one must be "born again" even to "see the kingdom of God" (John 3:3) and that "flesh and blood cannot inherit the kingdom of God" (1 Corinthians 15:50). Ignoring this biblical truth and following Augustine's error, Calvin determined (along with Guillaume Farel) to establish the kingdom of God on earth in Geneva, Switzerland.

On November 10, 1536, the Confession of Faith, which all the bourgeoisie and inhabitants of Geneva and subjects in its territories should swear to adhere to, and which Farel had drafted in consultation with Calvin, was officially presented to the city. It was a lengthy document with detailed rules covering everything from church membership, attendance, preaching, and obedience of the flock, to expulsion of offenders. Geneva's authorities approved the document on January 16, 1537. "In March the Anabaptists were banished. In April, at Calvin's instigation [a house-to-house inspection was launched] to ensure that the inhabitants subscribed to the Confession of Faith.... On October 30 there was an attempt to wring a profession of faith from all those hesitating. Finally, on November 12, an edict was issued declaring that all recalcitrants '[who] do not wish to swear to the Reformation are commanded to leave the city'...."[16]

"The Reformation"? There were variations and differences among the several factions in the budding Reformation, from Luther to Zwingli. But in Geneva, Calvinism alone was to be known as "The Reformation" and "Reformed Theology." That presumptuous claim is still insisted upon by Calvinists today all over the world.

Calvin's first attempt failed. Boettner acknowledges, "Due to an attempt of Calvin and Farel to enforce a too severe system of discipline in Geneva, it became necessary for them to leave the city temporarily."[17]

Calvin's Triumphant Return

Three years later, however, facing Catholic opposition from within and the threat of armed intervention by Roman Catholics from without, Geneva's city council decided that they needed Calvin's strong measures and invited him back. He reentered the city on September 13, 1541. This time, he would eventually succeed in imposing his version of the Reformation upon Geneva's citizens with an iron hand. His first act was to hand the city council his *Ecclesiastical Ordinances*, which were adopted November 20, 1541. Stefan Zweig tells us:

> One of the most momentous experiments of all time began when this lean and harsh man entered the Cornavian Gate [of Geneva]. A State [the walled city-state of Geneva] was to be converted into a rigid mechanism; innumerable souls, people with countless feelings and thoughts, were to be compacted into an all-embracing and unique system. This was the first [Protestant] attempt made in Europe to impose...a uniform subordination upon an entire populace.
>
> With systematic thoroughness, Calvin set to work for the realization of his plan to convert Geneva into the first Kingdom of God on earth. It was to be a community without corruption, disorder, vice or sin; it was to be the New Jerusalem, a centre from which the salvation of the world would radiate.... The whole of his life was devoted to the service of this one idea.[18]

Calvin's intention to establish ecclesiastical rule would occupy most of the rest of his life. Though recognizing Calvin's influence and power, the Small Council of Sixty and the Large

Council of Two Hundred, responsible for civil affairs, resisted being taken over by the religious authority (consistory) over which Calvin held sway. The power struggle continued for years, the councils even seeking to retain control over some church disciplines such as excommunications, with Calvin defiantly refusing to yield.

Finally, in February 1555, Calvin's supporters gained the absolute majority on the council. On May 16th there was an attempted uprising against Calvin's exclusion from the Lord's Supper of certain libertarian civic officials.[19] Riot leaders who fled Geneva to Bern were sentenced to death in absentia. Four who failed to escape were beheaded and quartered, and their body parts were hung in strategic locations as a warning.[20] Evoking the phrase "henchmen of Satan" that he had years before used against Anabaptists, Calvin justified this barbarity: "Those who do not correct evil when they can do so and their office requires it are guilty of it."[21]

From early 1554 until his death in 1564, "no one any longer dared oppose the Reformer openly."[22] Calvin's opponents had either been silenced, expelled, or had fled to save their lives. Calvin's "control of the city continued without weakening." He was determined to make Geneva the base for building Augustine's City of God everywhere. "Geneva became the symbol and incarnation of that 'other' Reformation...,"[23] but which Calvinists today claim was *the* Reformation.

Tyranny in Geneva

Perhaps Calvin thought he was God's instrument to force Irresistible Grace (a key doctrine in Calvinism) upon the citizens of Geneva, Switzerland—even upon those who proved their unworthiness by resisting to the death. He unquestionably did his best to be irresistible in imposing "righteousness," but what he imposed and the manner in which he imposed it was far from grace and the teachings and example of Christ.

Some of those who profess a "Reformed" faith today, especially those known as Reconstructionists such as the late Rousas J. Rushdoony, Gary North, Jay Grimstead, and others (including organizations such as the Coalition on Revival), take Calvin's Geneva as their model and thus hope to Christianize the United States and then the world. Many Christian activists of looser attachment to Calvin hope, in their own way, through protest marches and the organizing of large enough voting blocks, to force an ungodly American citizenry into godly living. No one ever worked so hard at attempting to do this and for so long a time as Calvin. Durant reports:

> To regulate lay conduct a system of domiciliary visits was established...and questioned the occupants on all phases of their lives.... The allowable color and quantity of clothing, and the number of dishes permissible at a meal, were specified by law. Jewelry and lace were frowned upon. A woman was jailed for arranging her hair to an immoral height....
>
> Censorship of the press was taken over from Catholic and secular precedents and enlarged: books... of immoral tendency were banned.... To speak disrespectfully of Calvin or the clergy was a crime. A first violation of these ordinances was punished with a reprimand, further violation with fines, persistent violation with imprisonment or banishment. Fornication was to be punished with exile or drowning; adultery,

> blasphemy, or idolatry, with death...a child was be-
> headed for striking its parents. In the years 1558–59
> there were 414 prosecutions for moral offenses; between
> 1542 and 1564 there were seventy-six banishments and
> fifty-eight executions; the total population of Geneva
> was then about 20,000.[24]

The oppression of Geneva could not have come from the Holy Spirit's guidance ("...where the Spirit of the Lord is, there is liberty" [2 Corinthians 3:17]), but rather from Calvin's powerful personality and extreme view of God's sovereignty that denied free will to man. Thus "grace" had to be irresistibly imposed in an unbiblical attempt to inflict "godliness" upon the citizens of Geneva. In contrast to the humility, mercy, love, compassion, and longsuffering of Christ, whom he loved and tried to serve, Calvin exerted authority much like the papacy he despised. Moreover, he criticized other Protestant leaders for not doing the same:

> Seeing that the defenders of the Papacy are so bitter and
> bold in behalf of their superstitions, that in their atro-
> cious fury they shed the blood of the innocent, it should
> shame Christian magistrates that in the protection of
> certain truth, they are entirely destitute of spirit.[25]

Calvin's defenders deny the facts and attempt to exonerate him by blaming what he did on the civil authorities. Boettner even insists that "Calvin was the first of the Reformers to demand complete separation between Church and State."[26] In fact, Calvin not only established ecclesiastical law, but he codified the civil legislation.[27] He held the civil authorities responsible to "foster and maintain the external worship of God, to defend sound doctrine and the condition of the church"[28] and to see that "no idolatry, no blasphemy against God's name, no calumnies against his truth, nor other offenses to religion break out and be disseminated among the people...[but] to prevent the true religion...from being with impunity openly violated and polluted by public blasphemy."[29]

Calvin used the civil arm to impose his peculiar doctrines upon the citizens of Geneva, and to enforce them. Zweig, who pored over the official records of the City Council for Calvin's day, tells us, "There is hardly a day, in the records of the settings of the Town Council, in which we do not find the remark: 'Better consult Master Calvin about this.'"[30] Pike reminds us that Calvin was given a "consultant's chair" in every meeting of the city authorities and "when he was sick the authorities would come to his house for their sessions."[31] Rather than diminishing with time, Calvin's power only grew. John McNeil, a Calvinist, admits that "in Calvin's latter years, and under his influence, the laws of Geneva became more detailed and more stringent."[32]

Don't Cross Dr. Calvin!

With dictatorial control over the populace ("he ruled as few sovereigns have done"[33]), Calvin imposed his brand of Christianity upon the citizenry with floggings, imprisonments, banishments, and burnings at the stake. Calvin has been called "the Protestant Pope" and "the Genevese dictator" who "would tolerate in Geneva the opinions of only one person, his own."[34] Concerning the adoption in Geneva of a confession of faith that was made mandatory for all citizens, the historian Philip Schaff comments:

> It was a glaring inconsistency that those who had just
> shaken off the yoke of popery as an intolerable bur-
> den, should subject their conscience and intellect to
> a human creed; in other words, substitute for the old
> Roman popery a modern Protestant popery.[35]

Durant says that "Calvin held power as the head of this
consistory; from 1541 till his death in 1564, his voice was the
most influential in Geneva."[36] Vance reminds us that:

> Calvin was involved in every conceivable aspect of city
> life: safety regulations to protect children, laws against
> recruiting mercenaries, new inventions, the introduc-
> tion of cloth manufacturing, and even dentistry. He
> was consulted not only on all important state affairs,
> but on the supervision of the markets and assistance
> for the poor.[37]

Calvin's efforts were often laudable, but matters of faith
were legislated as well. A confession of faith drawn up by Calvin
was made mandatory for all citizens. It was a crime for anyone
to disagree with this Protestant pope. Durant comments:

> All the claims of the popes for the supremacy of the
> church over the state were renewed by Calvin for his
> church....[Calvin] was as thorough as any pope in
> rejecting individualism of belief; this greatest legislator
> of Protestantism completely repudiated that principle
> of private judgment with which the new religion had
> begun.... In Geneva...those...who could not accept it
> would have to seek other habitats. Persistent absence
> from Protestant [Calvinist] services, or continued
> refusal to take the Eucharist was a punishable offense.

> Heresy again became...treason to the state, and was to
> be punished with death.... In one year, on the advice of
> the Consistory, fourteen alleged witches were sent to
> the stake on the charge that they had persuaded Satan
> to afflict Geneva with plague.[38]

Calvin was again following in the footsteps of Augustine, who had enforced "unity...through common participation in the Sacraments...."[39] A medical doctor named Jerome Bolsec dared to disagree with Calvin's doctrine of predestination. He was arrested for saying that "those who posit an eternal decree in God by which he has ordained some to life and the rest to death make of Him a tyrant...."[40] Bolsec was arrested and banished from Geneva with the warning that if he ever returned he would be flogged.[41] John Trolliet, a city notary, criticized Calvin's view of predestination for "making God the author of sin."[42] (In fact, the charge was true, as documented in chapters 9 and 10 of *What Love Is This?*) The court decreed that "thenceforward no one should dare to speak against this book [*Institutes*] and its doctrine."[43] So much for the freedom of conscience that had been promised would replace the popes' intolerable oppression!

Calvin's power was so great that it was tantamount to treason against the state to oppose him. A citizen named Jacques Gruet was arrested on suspicion of having placed a placard on Calvin's pulpit which read in part, "Gross hypocrite...! After people have suffered long, they avenge themselves.... Take care that you are not served like M. Verle [who had been killed]...."[44]

Gruet was tortured twice daily in a manner similar to which Rome, rightly condemned by the Reformers for doing so, tortured the victims of her inquisitions who were accused of daring

to disagree with her dogmas. The use of torture for extract-
ing "confessions" was approved by Calvin.[45] After thirty days of
severe suffering, Gruet finally confessed—whether truthfully, or
in desperation to end the torture, no one knows. On July 16,
1547, "half dead, he was tied to a stake, his feet were nailed to
it, and his head was cut off."[46] Beheading was the penalty for
civil crimes; burning at the stake was the penalty for *theological
heresy*. Here we see disagreement with Calvin was treated as a
capital offense against the *state*.

Irrational Behavior

Calvin followed the principles of punishment, coercion, and
death that Augustine had advocated. Concerning just one period
of panic in the face of plague and famine, Cottret describes "an
irrational determination to punish the fomenters of the evil."
He tells of a man who "died under torture in February 1545,
without admitting his crime…the body was dragged to the
middle of town, in order not to deprive the inhabitants of the
fine burning they had a right to. Sorcerers, like heretics…were
characterized by their combustible qualities…. The executions
continued. Yet those detained refused to confess; the tortures
were combined skillfully to avoid killing the guilty foolishly…
[some] were decapitated…. Some committed suicide in their
cells to avoid torture…. One of the arrested women threw
herself from a window…. Seven men and twenty-four women
died in the affair; others fled. "[47]

    In a letter, Calvin advised a friend: "The Lord tests us in
a surprising manner. A conspiracy has just been discovered of
men and women who for three years employed themselves in

spreading the plague in the city by means of sorcery.... Fifteen women have already been burned, and the men have been punished still more rigorously. Twenty-five of these criminals are still shut up in the prisons.... So far God has preserved our house."

Cottret continues: "Calvin therefore shares in all respects the fantasies of his entourage. He found occasion to exhort his contemporaries to pursue sorcerers in order to 'extirpate such a race'.... A pair of these henchmen of Satan had just been burned the previous month...."[48] Calvin even believed that the devil, on at least one occasion, helped rid Geneva of evil, "for in October 1546 he [the devil] bore away through the air (so Calvin himself testifies) a man who was ill with the plague, and who was known for his misconduct and impiety."[49]

Good Intentions Gone Astray

No one has ever been as successful as John Calvin at totalitarian imposition of "godliness" upon a whole society. And therefore, no one has proved as clearly as he that coercion cannot succeed because it can never change the *hearts* of men. Calvin's theology, as laid out in his *Institutes*, denied that unregenerate man could choose to believe and obey God. Apparently, he was ignorant of the commonsense fact that genuine choice is essential if man is to love and obey God or show love and real compassion to his fellows.

By his determined efforts to make Geneva's citizens obey, Calvin disproved his own theories of Unconditional Election and Irresistible Grace.

What he did prove, seemingly, by years of totalitarian

intimidation and force, was the first of Calvinism's Five Points, Total Depravity. Try as he might, there were many whom he simply could not persuade to live as he decreed, no matter how severe the penalty for failing to do so. He did succeed in creating many hypocrites who outwardly conformed to the law so long as the authorities were looking, but in their hearts longed for and practiced, when possible, the same old sins of the past.

Yes, there were reports from visitors that "cursing and swearing, unchastity, sacrilege, adultery, and impure living" such as were found elsewhere were absent from Geneva.[50] John Knox, of course, was enthusiastic. He called Geneva "the most perfect school of Christ that ever was in the earth since the days of the Apostles."[51] A visiting Lutheran minister, who thought Calvin's coercion was commendable, wrote in 1610, "When I was in Geneva I observed something great which I shall remember and desire as long as I live." He praised the "weekly investigations into the conduct, and even the smallest transgressions, of the citizens" and concluded, "If it were not for the difference of religion, I would have been chained to Geneva forever."[52]

Difference of religion? Yes, Calvinism was not Lutheranism, although both persecuted the Anabaptists. Protestantism involved several rival factions, to say nothing of millions of true Christians who had never given allegiance to Rome and thus had not come out of her as "Protestants." Untold multitudes of these believers had been martyred by Roman Catholics at the instigations of numerous popes for a thousand years before Luther and Calvin were born. Thus today's representation of Calvinism as "Reformation theology" that supposedly revived true Christianity is grossly inaccurate.

Admirers of John Calvin cite favorable stories as proof of

the godly influence he and his theories exerted in changing a godless society into one that honored God. His methods, however, often far from Christlike, could not be justified by *any* results. Nor could Calvin's means, as we have already noted, be justified by the fact that torture, imprisonment, and execution had been employed by Luther and the popes and other Roman Catholic clergy to force their religious views upon those under their power. A true follower of Christ is not to be conformed to this world but in his behavior is to follow Christ's example, no matter in what culture or time in history he finds himself.

Calvin's followers boast that he was the greatest of exegetes, who obeyed Scripture meticulously both in formulating his theology and in guiding his life. Supposedly, Calvin "was willing to break sharply with tradition where it was contrary to the Word of God."[53] At the same time, he is defended with the excuse that he was only conforming to the traditions long established by Rome, which began with Constantine. Otto Scott says, "In the early years of the Reformation, censorship of manners and morals remained a settled, accepted part of existing, ancient police regulations not only in Geneva, but in all Europe."[54]

This is true. Such curbs discouraged rebellious attempts to leave one's "class," etc. But that was not Christianity as taught and exemplified by Christ and His apostles.

There is no way to defend Calvin's conduct from Scripture. Yes, he was loving and caring toward those who agreed with him. Yes, he expended himself and shortened his life through visiting the sick, caring for the flock, and preaching continually. But in his treatment of those who disagreed with him, he did not follow but violated both the teachings and the example of Christ and His apostles.

The Hopelessness of Imposed "Godliness"

Sadly, in spite of threats and torture, Calvin's Geneva was not as righteous a city as the selected optimistic stories seem to indicate. The surviving records of the Council of Geneva unveil a city more similar to the rest of the world than Calvin's admirers like to admit. These documents reveal "a high percentage of illegitimate children, abandoned infants, forced marriages, and sentences of death."[55] The stepdaughter and son-in-law of Calvin were among the many condemned for adultery.[56] Calvin had done his best but had failed. He had not been able to produce among sinners the ideal society—Augustine's City of God—which he had envisioned when he wrote his *Institutes*.

Calvinists teach that the totally depraved unsaved can respond to God *only* in unbelief, rebellion, and opposition. White explains: "Unregenerate men who are enemies of God most assuredly respond to God: in a universally negative fashion."[57] That being the case, by his own theory, Calvin's efforts at Geneva were doomed before they began!

Speaking for most Calvinists, R. C. Sproul explains that according to the "Reformed view of predestination before a person can choose Christ he must be born again"[58] by a sovereign act of God. How could Calvin be sure that God had done this work in the hearts of all in Geneva? If God had not predestined every citizen of Geneva to salvation, then Calvin was wrong in trying to force them into a Christian mold. Yet coercion even by force was an integral part of the system as practiced by Calvin himself and his immediate successors.

If Calvinists today do not approve of such conduct, might not the Calvinism that produced such tyranny also be wrong in other respects?

How many of the "elect" were there in Geneva? As Jay Adams points out, no one, not even Calvin, could know. Calvinism has no explanation for how the elect could have been identified with certainty among the hypocrites who acted as though they were among the elect by behaving themselves, but did so only out of fear of the temporal consequences. No matter how hard Calvin tried, if God (according to Calvin's doctrine) had not elected every citizen in Geneva to salvation (and He apparently had not), then evil would still persist—though not as blatantly as in other cities of that day.

Considering Calvin's abysmal record of failure, one wonders why today's Reconstructionists, who hold to the same dogma, nevertheless believe they will be able to impose righteous living upon entire nations. Or why evangelicals continue to praise Calvin, the oppressor of Geneva.

Servetus: The Arch Heretic

Born Miguel Serveto in Villanova in 1511, the man known to the world as Michael Servetus "discovered the pulmonary circulation of the blood—the passage of the blood from the right chamber of the heart along the pulmonary artery to and through the lungs, its purification there by aeration, and its return via the pulmonary vein to the left chamber of the heart." He was in some ways "a bit more insane than the average of his time," announcing the end of the world in which "the Archangel Michael would lead a holy war against both the papal and Genevese Antichrists."[59]

Unquestionably, he was a rank heretic whose ravings about Christ reflected a combination of Islam and Judaism, both of which intrigued him. He was, however, right about some things: that God does not predestine souls to hell and that God is love. His otherwise outrageous ideas might have passed unnoticed had he not published them and attempted to force them upon Calvin and his fellow ministers in Geneva with aggressive, contemptuous, and blasphemous railings. That Servetus titled one of his published works *The Restitution of Christianity* could only be taken as an intentional personal affront by the author of the *Institutes of the Christian Religion*.

Servetus wrote at least thirty unwelcome letters to Calvin, which must have irritated the latter greatly. On February 13, 1546, Calvin wrote to Farel, "Servetus has just sent me a long volume of his ravings. If I consent he will come here, but I will not give my word, for should he come, if my authority is of any avail, I will not suffer him to get out alive."[60] Servetus made the mistake of passing through Geneva seven years later on his way to Naples and was recognized when he attended church (possibly out of fear of arrest for nonattendance) by someone who saw through his disguise and notified Calvin, who in turn ordered his arrest.

The Torture and Burning of Servetus

Early in the trial, which lasted two months, Calvin wrote to Farel, "I hope that sentence of death will be passed upon him."[61] Obviously, if the God one believes in predestines billions to a burning hell (all of whom He *could* rescue), then to burn at the stake a totally depraved heretic would seem quite mild and easily justifiable. That logic, however, seems somehow to escape many of today's evangelical Christians who admire the man and call themselves Calvinists.

The indictment, drawn up by Calvin the lawyer, contained thirty-eight charges supported by quotations from Servetus's writings. Calvin personally appeared in court as the accuser and as "chief witness for the prosecution."[62] Calvin's personal reports of the trial matched Servetus's railings with such epithets as "the dirty dog wiped his snout...the perfidious scamp soils each page with impious ravings," etc.[63]

Geneva's Council consulted the other churches of Protestant Switzerland, and six weeks later their reply was received: Servetus should be condemned but not executed. Nevertheless, under Calvin's leadership, He was sentenced to death on two counts of heresy: Unitarianism (rejection of the Trinity) and rejection of infant baptism. Durant gives the horrifying details:

> He asked to be beheaded rather than burned; Calvin was inclined to support this plea, but the aged Farel... reproved him for such tolerance; and the Council voted that Servetus should be burned alive.
>
> The sentence was carried out the next morning, October 17, 1553.... On the way [to the burning] Farel importuned Servetus to earn divine mercy by confessing the crime of heresy; according to Farel the condemned man replied, "I am not guilty, I have not merited death"; and he besought God to pardon his accusers. He was fastened to a stake by iron chains, and his last book was bound to his side. When the flames reached his face he shrieked with agony. After half an hour of burning he died.[64]

Calvin accused Servetus of "specious arguments" against infant baptism. But the latter's main objections (in spite of his other faults) were actually quite sound. Calvin's derisive response, purged of that unchristian "biting and mocking tone of ridicule that would never leave him"[65] is condensed as follows:

> Servetus [argues] that no man becomes our brother unless by the Spirit of adoption...only conferred by the hearing of faith.... Who will presume...that [God] may not ingraft infants into Christ by some other secret method...? Again he objects, that infants cannot be...begotten by the word. But what I have said again and again I now repeat...God takes his own methods of regenerating...to consecrate infants to himself, and initiate them by a sacred symbol.... Circumcision was common to infants before they received understanding.... Doubtless the design of Satan in assaulting paedobaptism with all his forces is to...efface, that attestation of divine grace...that from their birth they have been...acknowledged by him as his children.....[66]

In spite of his other false views, Servetus was correct in his objections to infant baptism and was therefore, in that respect, burned at the stake for a biblical belief that opposed Calvin's heresy of baptismal regeneration of infants practiced in many Calvinist churches to this day.

The Failure of Attempted Exonerations

Many attempts have been made by his modern followers to exonerate Calvin for the unconscionably cruel death of Michael Servetus. It is said that Calvin visited him in prison and pleaded with him to recant. At the same time, Calvin's willingness for Servetus to be beheaded rather than burned at the stake was not necessarily motivated by kindness, but was an attempt to transfer responsibility to the civil authority. Beheading was the penalty for civil crimes; burning at the stake was for heresy. The charges, however, were clearly theological, not civil, and were brought by Calvin himself.

The civil authority only acted at the behest of the church. According to the laws of Geneva, Servetus, as a traveler passing through, should have been expelled from the city, not executed. It was only his heresy that doomed him—and only because Calvin pressed the charges. Calvin did exactly what his view of God required, in keeping with what he had written to Farel seven years before.

Here again, over Calvin's shoulder, we see the long shadow of Augustine. To justify his actions, Calvin borrowed the same perverted interpretation of Luke 14:23 that Augustine had used. Frend said, "Seldom have gospel words been given so unexpected a meaning."[67] Farrar writes:

> To him [Augustine] are due...above all the bitter spirit of theological hatred and persecution. His writings became the Bible of the Inquisition. His name was adduced—and could there be a more terrible Nemesis on his errors?—to justify the murder of Servetus.[68]

There was wide acclaim from Catholics and Protestants alike for the burning of Servetus. The Inquisition in Vienna burned him in effigy. Melanchthon wrote Calvin a letter in which he called the burning "a pious and memorable example to all posterity" and gave "thanks to the Son of God" for the just "punishment of this blasphemous man." Others, however, disagreed; and Calvin became the target of criticism.

Many living in Calvin's time recognized the wickedness of using force to promote "Christianity." Full approval was lacking even among Calvin's closest friends.[69] Rebuking Calvin for the burning of Servetus, Chancellor Nicholas Zurkinden, a magistrate, said the sword was inappropriate for enforcing faith.[70] In spite of many such rebukes, Calvin insisted that the civil sword must keep the faith pure. His conduct was in line with his rejection of God's love toward all, and his denial of human choice to believe the gospel.

Calvin's Self-Justifications

Some critics argued that burning Servetus would only encourage the Roman Catholics of France to do the same to the Huguenots (70,000 would be slaughtered in one night in 1572). Stung by such opposition, in February 1554, Calvin published a broadside aimed at his critics: *Defensio orthodoxae fidei de sacra Trinitate contra prodigiosos errores Michaelis Serveti*. He argued that all who oppose God's truth are worse than murderers, because murder merely kills the body whereas heresy damns the soul for eternity (was that worse than predestination by God to eternal damnation?), and that God had explicitly instructed Christians to kill heretics and even to smite with the sword any city that abandoned the true faith:

> Whoever shall maintain that wrong is done to heretics and blasphemers in punishing them [with death] makes himself an accomplice in their crime.... It is God who speaks, and it is clear what law He would have kept in the Church even to the end of the world...so that we spare not kin nor blood of any, and forget all humanity when the matter is to combat for His glory.[71]

Historian R. Tudor Jones declares that this tract, which Calvin wrote in defense of the burning of Michael Servetus, "is Calvin at his most chilling...as frightening in its way as Luther's tract against the rebellious peasants."[72] Eight years later, Calvin was still defending himself against criticism and still advocating the burning of heretics. In a 1561 letter to the Marquis de Poet, high chamberlain to the King of Navarre, Calvin advises sternly:

> Do not fail to rid the country of those zealous scoundrels who stir up the people to revolt against us. Such monsters should be exterminated, as I have exterminated Michael Servetus the Spaniard.[73]

A year later (just two years before his own death), Calvin again justifies Servetus's death, while at the same time acknowledging that he was responsible: "And what crime was it of mine if our Council *at my exhortation*...took vengeance upon his execrable blasphemies (emphasis added)?"[74]

Calvinists today still persist in offering one excuse after another to exonerate their hero. Nevertheless, even such a staunch Calvinist as William Cunningham writes:

> There can be no doubt that Calvin beforehand, at the time, and after the event, explicitly approved and defended the putting him [Servetus] to death, and assumed the responsibility of the transaction.[75]

Does the Christian Life Conform to Culture?

Today Calvin's supporters complain, "No Christian leader has ever been so often condemned by so many. And the usual grounds for condemnation are the execution of Servetus and the doctrine of predestination."[76] In fact, Servetus was only one of many such victims of Calvinism carried to its logical conclusion. Defenders usually plead that what Calvin did was common practice and that he should be judged by the standard of his time. Are "new creatures in Christ Jesus" to rise no higher than the conventions of their culture and their moment in history? Surely not!

God's sovereignty in controlling and causing everything that occurs is the very heart of Calvinism. Staunch Calvinist C. Gregg Singer declares that "the secret grandeur of Calvin's theology lies in his grasp of the biblical teaching of the sovereignty of God."[77] Could Calvin truly have believed that he was God's instrument chosen from past eternity to coerce, torture, and kill in order to force Geneva's citizens into behavior that God had predestined and would *cause?*

Calvin has been acclaimed as a godly example who based his theology and actions upon Scripture alone. But much that he did was unbiblical in the extreme, though consistent with his theology. Is not that fact sufficient reason to examine Calvinism carefully from Scripture? That the Pope and Luther joined in unholy alliances with civil rulers to imprison, flog, torture, and kill dissenters in the name of Christ does not justify Calvin. Is it not possible that some of Calvin's theology was just as unscriptural as the principles that drove his conduct? William Jones declares:

> And with respect to Calvin, it is manifest, that…the most hateful feature in all the multiform character of popery adhered to him through life—I mean the *spirit of persecution*.[78]

Is not Christ alone the standard for His followers? And is He not always the same, unchanged by time or culture? How can the popes be *condemned* (and rightly so) for the evil they did under the banner of the Cross, while Calvin is *excused* for doing much the same, though on a smaller scale? The following are just two passages among many that condemn Calvin:

- But the wisdom that is from above is first pure, then peaceable, gentle, and easy to be intreated, full of mercy and good fruits, without partiality, and without hypocrisy. (James 3:17)

- He that saith he abideth in him [Christ] ought himself also so to walk, even as he [Christ] walked. (1 John 2:6)

One wonders how so many of today's Christian leaders can continue to laud a man whose behavior was often so far removed from the biblical exemplar reflected above.

WHEN GRACE ... ISN'T

WHAT CALVIN PRACTICED in imposing his Augustinian doctrine upon those who disagreed was in many instances far from Christianity and God's grace. It was, however, consistent with his view of *Irresistible* Grace and a God who sovereignly imposes it upon the elect.

If Calvinism were true, how else could God make certain that the blood of Christ, shed on the cross for sin, would actually bring salvation to the elect? How could a "totally depraved" sinner be made to believe, except irresistibly? In his dispute with Rome, Calvin insisted that "divine grace [acts] irresistibly...." [1]

White argues that because the Bible says *Christ saves* sinners, we can't change it to say that he "saves synergistically with the assistance of the sinner himself." [2] Simply *believing* the gospel and *receiving* its free gift of salvation, however, could hardly qualify as "assistance" to God. Yet Pink likewise argues:

> What impression is made upon the minds of
> those men of the world who, occasionally, attend
> a Gospel service...? Is it not that a *disappointed*
> God is the One whom Christians believe in? From
> what is heard from the average evangelist today,
> is not any serious hearer *obliged* to conclude that
> he professes to represent a God who is filled with
> benevolent intentions, yet unable to carry them
> out; that He is earnestly desirous of blessing men,
> but that they will not let Him?[3]

Has Pink forgotten that much of the Old Testament was
written by weeping prophets who expressed God's disappoint-
ment and grief over Israel's rejection of His love and grace and
proffered mercy? Nevertheless, to the Calvinist, if salvation is
merely an offer that man can refuse, that puts man in charge
rather than God. This argument is foolish. The recipient of a
gift can only accept or reject what is offered. To sovereignly
impose either a gift or love would destroy both. Man is *not* in
charge. If he doesn't turn to God willingly with his whole heart,
he is eternally doomed.

Calvin's mistaken belief that God's sovereignty would be
destroyed by free will necessitated a God who elected some to
salvation and predestined the rest of mankind to eternal hell.
No human could have any choice in the matter. That abhor-
rent doctrine directly contradicts the hundreds of scriptures
in which God calls upon all men to repent, to believe, and to
receive eternal life as a gift of His grace. Calvinism blinds its
followers to such scriptures. Thus Pink mourns:

> It is sad indeed to find one like the late Dr. [A. T.]
> Pierson—whose writings are generally so scriptural
> and helpful—saying, "It is a tremendous thought that

even God Himself cannot...prevent me from defying and denying Him, and would not exercise His power in such a direction if He could, and could not if He would" (*A Spiritual Clinique*). It is sadder still to discover that many other respected and loved brethren are giving expression to the same sentiments. Sad, because directly at variance with the Holy Scriptures."[4]

In fact, Calvinism is "at variance with the Holy Scriptures."

God the Puppet Master

The insistence upon a sovereignty that necessarily disallows any choice to man became the foundation of that system of theology known as Calvinism today. God's sovereignty and man's inability to say, think, or do anything that God had not predestined has been the continuing emphasis, reducing man to a puppet with God pulling the strings.

Engelsma asserts, "The Apostle Paul was an avowed, ardent predestinarian, holding double predestination, election, and reprobation."[5] What Engelsma attributes to Paul, Jewett claims was the common belief of every theologian in history worth mentioning: "Every theologian of the first rank from Augustine to Barth has affirmed...that God's election is a righteous and holy decision that he makes according to his own good pleasure to redeem the objects of his electing love."[6] Man cannot even believe the gospel without God *causing* him to do so. And that He causes so few to believe and predestines so many to eternal torment is "according to his own good pleasure"! Is this really the "God and Father of our Lord Jesus Christ" (Ephesians 1:3)?

Piper writes an entire book "to defend the claim that God is not unrighteous in unconditionally predestining some Israelites to salvation and some to condemnation."[7]

What are we to make of God's pleadings with *all* Israel to repent? And what of the fact that *all* Israel killed the lamb, sprinkled the blood, were delivered from Egypt, ate the manna, and "did all drink the same spiritual drink...that spiritual Rock that followed them: and that Rock was Christ" (1 Corinthians 10:4)? Yet God predestined many if not most of them to eternal condemnation? On the contrary, it was clear tht God desired the eternal salvation of *all* Israel.

We have no disagreement with Calvinism concerning God's righteousness or His justice—the issue is His love. Does He love the whole world and desire all men to be saved, or doesn't He? Calvinism limits God's infinite love to a select group; the Bible declares His love for all—and allows man the choice that love requires.

Packer explains the Calvinist position: "God loves all in some ways (everyone whom he creates...receives many undeserved good gifts...). He loves some in all ways (that is...He brings them to faith, to new life and to glory according to his predestinating purpose)."[8] But would it really be love "in some ways" for God to give temporary, earthly "undeserved good gifts" to those He has predestined to eternal torment? Love "in some ways"? Absolutely not! Love cannot stop short of giving all it possibly could to those who are loved.

What love is this that provides *temporal blessings* for those it predestines to *eternal doom*?" Christ said it was a bad bargain for a man to "gain the whole world, and lose his own soul" (Matthew 16:26). Thus it could not be love of *any kind* for

God to give even "the whole world" to one whom He had pre-destined to "lose his own soul"! Yet Packer calls it a gift of the "love" that Calvinism attributes to God. Palmer declares:

> By the decree of God, for the manifestation of His glory, some men and angels are predestinated to everlasting life; and others foreordained to everlasting death.... God has appointed the elect to glory.... The rest of mankind God was pleased, according to the unsearchable counsel of His own will...for the glory of His sovereign power over His creatures...to ordain them to dishonor and wrath for their sin, to the praise of His glorious justice.[9]

How can we fail to denounce such a horrifying misrepresentation of God? Calvinism is driven to this God-dishonoring belief by its misunderstanding of sovereignty. And the solution is so simple: acknowledge that God sovereignly gave to man a genuine power of choice, and God is exonerated and honored.

A One-Sided Emphasis

Calvinism's continual emphasis is upon God's sovereignty, glory, justice, and wrath. Searching its literature, one finds very little, if anything, of God's mercy, grace, compassion, and love for anyone but the elect.

Irresistible Grace is a human invention imposed upon the Bible. White writes, " 'Irresistible grace' is a reference to God's sovereign regeneration of His elect: any other use of this phrase is in error."[10] He insists upon precise rules for handling a phrase that isn't even found in the Bible—a concept about which Paul and the other apostles obviously knew nothing.

When Moses asked for a revelation of God's glory, the response was, "I will make all my goodness pass before thee... [and] the LORD passed by before him, and proclaimed, The LORD, The LORD God, merciful and gracious, longsuffering, and abundant in goodness and truth, Keeping mercy for thousands, forgiving iniquity and transgression and sin, and that will by no means clear [i.e., forgive without the penalty being paid] the guilty...(Exodus 33:19; 34:6–7).

Calvinism places great emphasis upon God's statement, "[I] will be gracious to whom I will be gracious, and will shew mercy on whom I will shew mercy" (Exodus 33:19)—but always from the negative point of view, as though God were pronouncing limitations upon His grace and mercy, when He is actually declaring their limitless expanse. Piper writes, "In dispensing mercy and grace God is dependent on nothing but his own free and sovereign choice."[11]

That is true, but God declares repeatedly that His grace and mercy are for all. The Calvinist, however, sees in God's declaration to Moses a limiting of grace and mercy to the elect, whereas the whole tenor of Scripture tells us that His mercy and grace are boundless. The entire context of this passage requires the understanding that God is revealing the infinite expanse of His mercy and grace, and not its limitations—while at the same time making it clear that grace does not compromise justice: "and that will by no means clear the guilty" (Exodus 34:7).

A Continuing Cover-Up

Is it possible that Calvin's tyrannical influence over Geneva, which was often so un-Christlike, was a direct result of his view of God as a harsh Sovereign more ready to condemn than to save? Tragically, that view of God persists among many Calvinists today.

Calvinists have avoided the truth about John Calvin the man. The booklet put out by John Piper and his pastoral staff at Bethlehem Baptist Church in Minneapolis opens with "Historical Information." It begins, "John Calvin, the famous theologian and pastor of Geneva...."[12]—and that is it for the "historical information." There is not one word of the oppressive behavior of this "Protestant Pope," which we have documented. Is it really fair to readers to praise Calvin without telling the truth? Doesn't that give a false impression? Isn't Calvin's conduct as important as his theology? Aren't the two ultimately related?

In a more recent book, Piper purports to tell the truth faithfully about Augustine, Luther, and Calvin, whom he calls "three famous and flawed fathers in the Christian church..." and thereby to show how "the faithfulness of God triumphs over the flaws of men."[13] Piper declares that his aim in this book "is that the glorious Gospel of God's all-satisfying, omnipotent grace will be savored, studied and spread for the joy of all peoples—in a never-ending legacy of Sovereign Joy."[14] *All peoples*—including the multitudes predestined to destruction? Can he be serious? And *Sovereign Joy*? What is that?

Calvinism's gospel of "omnipotent grace will be savored, studied and spread for the joy" of the non-elect, who have been foreordained to eternal doom and born into this world without any hope of changing their fate? What mockery! Yet the Calvinist seems blind to what his theory has done to the God who *is love* and to how it destroys any sense of urgency and responsibility to preach the gospel.

Piper reminds us that "The standard text on theology that Calvin and Luther drank from was *Sentences* by Peter Lombard. Nine-tenths of this book consists of quotations from Augustine.... Luther was an Augustinian monk, and Calvin immersed himself in the writings of Augustine, as we can see from the increased use of Augustine's writings in each new edition of the *Institutes*...paradoxically, one of the most esteemed fathers of the Roman Catholic Church 'gave us the Reformation.'" [15] Piper considers this paradox to be good; we do not, and for the many reasons we are giving—among them Rome's heresies that were carried over into the Reformation by Luther and Calvin. Why have I been so harshly criticized for pointing out the very "Catholic connection" that Piper admits?

His supposed exposé of Calvin's "flaws" is almost a whitewash. Piper admits that "fifteen women were burned at the stake" and that there were some cruelties. The full truth, as we have seen, is far worse. All is largely excused, however, as "Calvin's accommodation to brutal times" (as though Christians have no higher standard than current custom) and as having been done "in tribute and defense of Protestant martyrs in France." [16] Piper writes:

> The worst was his joining in the condemnation of the heretic, Michael Servetus, to burning at the stake in Geneva.... Calvin argued the case against him. He was sentenced to death. Calvin called for a swift execution, instead of burning, but he was burned at the stake on October 27, 1553.
>
> This has tarnished Calvin's name so severely that many cannot give his teaching a hearing. But it is not clear that most of us, given that milieu, would not have

> acted similarly under the circumstances...the times
> were harsh, immoral, and barbarous and had a con-
> taminating effect on everyone.... There was in the life
> and ministry of John Calvin a grand God-centeredness,
> Bible-allegiance, and iron constancy.
>
> Under the banner of God's mercy to miserable
> sinners, we would do well to listen and learn.... The
> conviction behind this book is that the glory of God,
> however dimly, is mirrored in the flawed lives of his
> faithful servants.[17]

With those sweet words, Piper really means that "under the
banner of God's mercy to *some* miserable sinners," the favored
elect may "listen and learn." But the non-elect can't listen and
learn; they are totally depraved and without understanding or
hope, because Piper's "God" keeps them in blindness! And even
if they could understand the message and wanted to believe, it
would not be possible, because they have been damned from
eternity past by an immutable decree of the Almighty. Is it
really fair to readers to give such a false impression of "sovereign" joy to "all peoples"?

And was it really "a grand God-centeredness, Bible-
allegiance, and iron constancy" that produced the ungodly and
unbiblical tyranny under Calvin at Geneva? Review Chapter 5
to see how Calvin is being protected by Piper. There were *doz-
ens* of others burned at the stake, not just Servetus, and there
were many Christians who did not practice torture and burning
at the stake in Calvin's day, thus proving that no one needed to
make "accommodation to brutal times." Would Paul have, or
John, or Christ? Why Calvin?

Could it be that Calvin's view of God (as taking pleasure in

damning billions He *could* save) fit right in with the "harshness
of the times"? Given Calvin's doctrine, no "accommodation to
brutal times" was necessary.

And why doesn't Piper explain that the reason Calvin
pushed for beheading was because that type of execution was
for civil crimes, and the onus would not be on himself? But
the charges pressed against Servetus by Calvin in court were
theological and required the flames. Calvin was simply trying to
circumvent the law. Do we praise him for that? Eight years later,
Calvin was still advising other rulers to exterminate heretics
"like I exterminated Michael Servetus..."! Calvin was a victim
of his times? No, a victim of his theology!

WILL CALVIN'S KINGDOM COME TODAY?

IN LIKE MANNER TO John Calvin's unbiblical tactics to "take dominion" over Geneva, Switzerland, increasing numbers of Christians are engaging in social and political activism for the astonishing purpose of attempting to coerce an ungodly society into adopting Christian standards of conduct.

"Operation Rescue" is one example. Its founder, Randall Terry [who converted to Roman Catholicism in 2006], explains that its purpose is to create social upheaval and thereby pressure government into changing the abortion laws. A typical brochure declares, "Rescues help produce the social tension necessary for political change...whether for good or bad, political change comes after groups of Americans bring enough tension to the nation and pressure on politicians that the laws are changed."

No matter how commendable the goal of such tactics, *there is not one example in the entire Bible* of political or social activism ever being advocated or used by God's people. That fact must weigh heavily upon any consideration of this important topic. There are numerous cases of *civil disobedience* in Scripture, but it was *never* engaged in for the purpose of forcing an ungodly society to obey biblical principles. The Hebrew midwives, for example, disobeyed Pharaoh's edict and spared the lives of the male babies, even lying to cover up their "rescue operation." God was so pleased with their obedience to Him that their names, Shiphrah and Puah, have been preserved for us (Exodus 1:15-22). This was, however, a matter of *individual conscience* before God, *not* an organized attempt to pressure the pagan Egyptians by mass demonstrations into adopting Israel's God-given morals.

The same is true of Shadrach, Meshach and Abednego's refusal to obey the king's command to bow to an idol, and of Daniel's defiance of the royal decree against prayer. Though boldly witnessing for God even to kings, Daniel *never* used his high government position to attempt to pressure a pagan society to abandon its evil practices to begin a godly way of life. Nor did Joseph or Esther pressure the pagan societies, in which they held high positions, to adopt biblical morals. So it was with Ezra and Nehemiah. They used their influence with kings to obtain permission to rebuild Jerusalem and the temple, but made no attempt to change the practices of those societies though they practiced abortion, homosexuality, and other evils.

There are no *biblical examples* to support today's "Christian activism." Christ "*suffered* for us, leaving us *an example that ye should follow his steps.*" He sternly and repeatedly rebuked

Israel's false religious leaders, yet He never spoke out—*not even once*—against the injustices of Roman civil authority! Nor did He advocate, organize, or engage in any public protests to pressure Rome into changing its corrupt system, or the society of His day its evil ways. He submitted to unjust authorities as Romans 13 tells us we should do today: "Who, when he was reviled, reviled not again; when he suffered, he threatened not; but committed himself to him that judgeth righteously" (1 Peter 2:21-25). No "activism" here! So it was with the apostles and the early church.

Yes, Paul told the centurion, who was about to have him unlawfully scourged, that he was a Roman citizen; and he told the local officials at Philippi to come and apologize for beating him and Silas without trial. That was not, however, political/ social activism. He was not attempting thereby to change society. He was simply standing up for his personal rights under the law (as we also should do), and that includes voting. Paul was determined to obey God rather than men and never held back from preaching the gospel, though it meant his life. If Christian activism is God's will, Paul would have been the first to pursue it fearlessly at whatever cost.

Scripture, then, from Genesis to Revelation, offers neither example nor doctrinal teaching to support the idea that Christians ought to engage in political/social activism, lobbying, the takeover methods of Coalition on Revival—or that Christians in public office could or should influence society to adopt biblical standards of conduct. Don't forget, any change would have to be effected through a corrupt political system involving an ungodly majority above and below. Romans 13 tells us to obey rulers, and 1 Timothy 2 to pray for them—not to attempt to change them by coercion. It is not only foolish but counterproductive to attempt to persuade the unsaved to live like Christians. They can't do it—and if they could it would only blind them the more to their sin and need of a Savior.

Acts 19:23-41 tells how a large group of citizens in Ephesus staged a huge "demonstration" against Paul and the gospel he preached. A crowd of probably several thousand persons tore their clothes, threw dust in the air and for two hours vociferously chanted their praise to the locally manufactured god that was their chief source of income."Great is Diana of the Ephesians!" they cried. Should Paul have gathered a larger crowd of Christians to cry out yet more loudly and longer and thereby impose their will upon the local authorities? Of course not! Such un-Christian conduct is demeaning of our Lord and His gospel and would have been unthinkable for the early church. Yet that is basically what Christian activism involves today—the well-meaning but foolish attempt to force "Christian principles" upon a godless society through more effective lobbying, larger demonstrations and greater social upheaval than the homosexuals, abortionists or pornographers can produce.

Rather than pressure the ungodly to live like saints, we must win them to Christ that they might live wholly by God. Our *personal lives* must be lived in obedience to God's laws even if that brings us into conflict with civil laws. In addition to avoiding idolatry and immorality, Christians must *preach the gospel* to everyone everywhere, regardless of government edicts to the contrary. In so doing, the apostles made that historic declaration: "We ought to obey God rather than men" (Acts 5:29)! Their example has been followed by Christians down through the centuries, from the martyrs under pagan Rome and its successor, Roman Catholicism, to those who smuggle Bibles into Islamic or communist lands.

Though forbidden by the authorities, the apostles persisted in preaching the gospel. Like their Lord, however, they made no attempt to lobby in Rome for an end to prostitution and abortions; nor did they stage public demonstrations for a change in unjust laws. There is a danger of being so caught up in the social aspect of good causes that one forgets and neglects the chief Christian calling. The Great Commission does not involve exerting a Christian influence upon society. We are not to "change society," but to "convert individuals." There is much talk today about "changing the world for Christ." In fact there is no biblical teaching or example to support that popular slogan. Rather than persuading sinners to live like saints, we must call them to heavenly citizenship through "repentance toward God and faith in our Lord Jesus Christ" (Acts 20:21).

But aren't we supposed to be "salt and light" in the world (Matthew 5:13-16)? Yes, Christ said so. To understand what He meant, we must look to Him as our perfect example. Jesus, "the light of the world," never advocated or tried to effect social/ political change. His *light* reveals sin and leads men to salvation, fitting them for heaven (Ephesians 5:8-13). *Salt* purifies the wound that light reveals and reproves.

Significant changes in society have been effected by preaching and example. Nevertheless, the abolition of slavery, the enactment of child labor laws and greater rights for women, while improvements to be thankful for, have not made society any more godly. Nor is it any more likely under these better conditions that a higher percentage of mankind will end up in heaven than before. While such changes are worth working for, many who call themselves Christians have become so absorbed in good causes that they have lost their fervor for saving souls. They have ended up joining forces with non-Christians who also espouse "traditional values" and in promoting a compromised "social gospel" that cannot save.

Yet the good that social/political activism often produces is a strong motivation for engaging in it. Many Christians were involved in the civil rights movement that finally ended segregation. Surely it is not wrong for Christians to engage in such activities! Certainly the innocent babies that are being murdered in abortion clinics, just as the Jews were in Nazi extermination camps, ought to be rescued! Should Christians do nothing? Is there no basis in Scripture for helping those who are downtrodden?

Yes, the Bible warns us: "If thou forbear to deliver them that are drawn unto death, and those that are ready to be slain; if thou sayest, Behold, we knew it not; doth not he that pondereth the heart consider it? and he that keepeth thy soul, doth not he know it? and shall not he render to every man according to his works?" (Proverbs 24:11-12). The parable of the good Samaritan, too, tells us that we ought to care for all those who are in need of help, even as Christ commands: "Do unto others as you would have them do unto you." These principles come under God's law written in the consciences of all mankind: "Love your neighbor as yourself" (Mark 12:31).

We ought to do all we can to rescue babies who are being aborted, just as we would seek to rescue anyone in danger. The Bible doesn't tell us what individual saints may have done in this regard because it is not specifically a Christian task nor is it something that has been assigned to the church, but is the responsibility of every person. Moreover, "rescues" should be engaged in to save lives—not for the purpose of creating "social upheaval" to coerce an evil society into adopting biblical standards....

Today's Christian activism is far too narrow and selective. It addresses certain issues but ignores many others of equal or greater importance. We must not only rescue the unborn but the children in public schools who are being perverted through the teaching of immorality, witchcraft, and occultism. We must identify psychology as the major vehicle of so much of this evil, and root it out of our churches, seminaries and universities.

We must denounce sin, call for national repentance, and preach the gospel in convicting power. Christians must call for repentance not only for homosexuality, child abuse, pornography and abortion but for more subtle forms of rebellion against God and rejection of Christ. The church must be indicted both for its lack of social concern and for its heresies and failure to preach the truth. We must denounce the destructive false teachings that abound. It is hypocritical for the church to protest the world's sins while tolerating and even honoring within its ranks those who preach a false gospel and are the enemies of the cross of Christ.

Instead of protesters we need prophets who call the world to repentance: Enochs who walk with God and warn of judgment (Hebrews 11:55; Jude 14-15); Noahs, preachers of righteousness (2 Peter 2:5), who warn of judgment to come and invite sinners into an ark of safety. What if, instead of building the ark, Noah had tried to reform society! We need Daniels: "Mene, mene, tekel upharsin"—the handwriting is on the wall, America! You've been weighed in the balance and found wanting! Murdered babies, the abomination of homosexuality, and society's flippant, deliberate rebellion against God have aroused His anger beyond any possibility of reprieve! We need Isaiahs and Jeremiahs who had never heard of making a "positive confession" or of the "power of positive or possibility thinking," but preached truth!

Like John Calvin's failed experiment to "Christianize" Geneva, "Christian activism" is not Christian. It represents a detour from the straight path the church is to walk before the world. It can confuse the real issues, lead to compromise and unholy alliances, and divert time and effort that would better be used in proclaiming the gospel. Weigh the demands upon your time and set priorities. Be fully engaged in rescuing souls for eternity.

Originally titled, "Christian Activism: Is It Biblical?"
The Berean Call, *November, 1989*

THE HOPE OF HIS CALLING

TOWARD THE END OF THE 1980s there was great
enthusiasm and confidence among many Christian leaders that
the world would be evangelized by the end of the year 2000.
Numerous programs targeted that seemingly propitious date. In
ecumenical fervor, evangelicals and Catholics joined together in
a "new evangelization" that would supposedly present to Christ
a world more Christian than not at the beginning of the new
millennium. As anyone would realize who heeded Scripture,
it wouldn't happen—and it didn't. The world is more pagan
today than ever, and the "third millennium of Christianity,"
so highly touted, is daily more apostate. The attempt to make
Christianity popular has perverted it.

Yes, history has seen times of apparent great revival—not
as a result, however, of Christianity's popularization, but in
the face of fierce opposition and severe persecution. Author

Wesley Brady writes, "On innumerable occasions, the meetings of the Wesleys, Whitefield and other itinerant preachers were attacked by drunken, brawling rabbles armed with...clubs, whips, clods, bricks, staves, stones...and rotten eggs. Sometimes they procured a bull and drove it into the midst of an open-air congregation; sometimes they contented themselves by producing noise with bells, horns, drums and pans to drown out the preacher's voice...and not infrequently they expended their fury in burning or tearing down the houses, and destroying or stealing the...possessions of the preacher's followers.

"John Wesley [sometimes] narrowly escaped with his life... while Whitefield, covered with blood...was rescued in the nick of time from the brutal fury of an Irish crowd at Dublin.... Without regard to age or sex, [the persecutors] pelted whole congregations with showers of dirt and stones. Many they beat mercilessly with clubs." (*England: Before and After Wesley*, p. 106). Before his death, however, Wesley saw great fruit from his labors as he presented the gospel in the power of the Holy Spirit. To a large extent, England became a nation that loved Christ and sent missionaries to the ends of the earth.

Today, however, England is in a sorrier state than before Wesley and Whitefield. Larger numbers now worship in mosques than in Christian churches. Holland, once a stronghold of morally austere Calvinism, is heedless of God and attracts billions of dollars in tourist trade by its licensed brothels and legalized homosexual and lesbian marriages.

The Dalai Lama was welcomed into the pulpit in Geneva, Switzerland, where John Calvin used to preach to what many thought (and some still imagine) was the ideal Christian society. The cathedral's dean, William McComish, General Treasurer of the World Alliance of Reformed Churches, called the Dalai Lama "His Holiness," praised his "spirituality" and declared that Calvin's cathedral was "becoming a home for a new religious centre to experience understanding between the world's major faiths."

The same downward path has been observed in the United States. In their beginnings, for example, the YWCA and YMCA were truly Christian; they are anything but Christian today. All of America's first universities were Christian: Harvard, Yale, Princeton, Brown, Dartmouth, the University of Pennsylvania, etc. Today they are not only atheistic but anti-Christian.

Harvard was founded in 1636 to train evangelical ministers. Its divinity school is now headed by a Roman Catholic priest and prides itself on being open to anything—except evangelical Christianity. With 18,000 students, an endowment of $13 billion and an annual income of $1.6 billion, Harvard is now a bastion of liberalism, pro-abortionism, radical feminism, relativism and militant anti-Christian rhetoric.

Yet not only Reconstructionists but most charismatics and many evangelicals are still boasting that Christianity is growing stronger through a last-days great revival and will eventually take over the world. Yes, it will, but it will be a false "Christianity" headed by Antichrist in partnership with the Vatican—the woman riding the beast of Revelation 17. One would have to be both spiritually and physically blind not to see this rapidly growing development, exactly as the Bible foretells it.

True Christianity was never intended to take over the world but to call out for heavenly citizenship those who would heed the gospel. Christ's solemn question, "when the Son of man cometh, shall he find [the true] faith on the earth?" (Luke 18:8) hardly promises a growing, much less dominant, Christianity in the last days. Instead, only a "little flock" will inherit the kingdom (Luke 12:32), having entered through that "strait gate" along the narrow way "which leadeth unto life, and few there be that find it" (Matthew 7:14). These are the "faithful in Christ Jesus" (Ephesians 1:1; Colossians 1:2; 2 Timothy 2:2; Revelation 17:14, etc.) and hated by the world (John 17:14).

Today, persecution of true believers in much of the world is far more prevalent than in Wesley's time, with more martyrs for Christ in the twentieth century than in the previous nineteen. Is that cause for discouragement? No. In fact, Christ said, "Blessed are ye, when men shall revile you, and persecute you, and shall say all manner of evil against you falsely, for my sake. Rejoice, and be exceeding glad: for great is your reward in heaven: for so persecuted they the prophets which were before you....Rejoice ye in that day, and leap for joy: for, behold, your reward is great in heaven..." (Matthew 5:11-12; Luke 6:23).

Our hope and our inheritance is not in this world, for we are "partakers of the heavenly calling" (Hebrews 3:1). As Christ told the first disciples, "If ye were of the world, the world would love his own: but because ye are not of the world, but I have chosen you out of the world, therefore the world hateth you.... The servant is not greater than his Lord. If they have persecuted me, they will also persecute you..." (John 15:19, 20). In our travels in Eastern Europe in Iron Curtain days we were asked by Christians why they were being persecuted when Christianity seemed to be so popular in America. A good question!

The best antidote to the mistaken beliefs that keep so many of today's Christians oriented toward an imagined conquest of this world is found in Paul's prayer for the Ephesian believers: "That the God of our Lord Jesus Christ, the Father of glory, may give unto you the spirit of wisdom and revelation in the knowledge of him: the eyes of your understanding being enlightened; that ye may know what is the hope of his calling, and what the riches of the glory of his inheritance in the saints, and what is the exceeding greatness of his power to usward who believe, according to the working of his mighty power, which he wrought in Christ, when he raised him from the dead..." (Ephesians 1:17-20).

And what is "the hope of his calling" to which Paul referred? Peter tells us very clearly: "But the God of all grace, who hath called us unto his eternal glory by Christ Jesus, after that ye have suffered a while, make you perfect, stablish, strengthen, settle you" (1 Peter 5:10). Our calling which we have in and through Christ Jesus is unto God's *eternal glory!* Nothing could compare with that! What could it mean and how is it possible?

God created man "in his own image, in the image of God created he him..." (Genesis 1:27). It was, of course, in His spiritual image, not in a physical image, for "God is a Spirit" (John 4:24). The wonder, happiness and perfection of the relationship Adam and Eve enjoyed reflected a heavenly love, patience, compassion, goodness, generosity, grace, mercy, peace, gentleness, selflessness, meekness—the very character of their Creator lived out in His creatures. Nothing to compare with the pure love and rapturous companionship these two daily experienced has thereafter been seen on earth!

Then sin entered that garden, bringing death (Romans 5:12). That beautiful relationship between Adam and Eve, and between them and their Creator, was destroyed. Adam blamed Eve, Cain murdered Abel, and humanity has gone downhill ever since. The glorious image of God in which man had been created was marred. Thus sin is defined as coming "short of the glory of God" (Romans 3:23). The glory of God's character once expressed so beautifully through the first man and woman became a receding memory that must have haunted them with a remorse which we cannot even begin to understand.

Christ is called, in the precise language of Scripture, "the second man." There was no one after Adam's fall who deserved to be called a "man" until "the man Christ Jesus" (1 Timothy 2:5) came into this world in a body prepared for Him (Hebrews 10:5) in the womb of the virgin Mary. When Pilate led Christ forth and pronounced to the mob, "Behold the man!" (John 19:5) he did not realize what he was saying. Here was God's perfect man! The "second man is the Lord from heaven" (1 Corinthians 15:47)! And He brings from glory to a fallen race the hope of glory, for through His death for our sins the image of God can be restored.

Again in the rigorous parlance of God's Word, Jesus is called "the last Adam" (1 Corinthians 15:45). Yes, He is the second Adam, but He is also the last. There will never be a third or fourth, etc. He is not only the progenitor of a new race of born-again believers. Christ is God's final solution. Sin will never mar God's new creation.

The first man, Adam, was made in the image of God but lost that likeness through the sin of rebellion. The second man, the last Adam, bears that image in a permanent perfection that the first Adam could not know. The man Christ Jesus is "the brightness of his [God's] glory, the express image of his person" (Hebrews 1:3). Just as the descendants of the first Adam inherited his warped and defiled image, so those who become

Christ's descendants by faith will be brought into His Father's house in His perfect and glorious image! Those who receive Christ have been predestinated by God "to be conformed to the image of his Son, that he might be the firstborn among many brethren" (Romans 8:29).

Christ, having paid the penalty for all sin and thereby having "[taken] away the sin of the world" (John 1:29), has "abolished death, and hath brought life and immortality to light through the gospel" (2 Timothy 1:10). "For as in Adam all [of his descendants] die, even so in Christ shall all [of His descendants] be made alive" (1 Corinthians 15:22). He will bring "many sons into glory" (Hebrews 2:10) "in the likeness of his resurrection" (Romans 6:5). "For our conversation [citizenship] is in heaven; from whence also we look for the Saviour, the Lord Jesus Christ: who shall change our vile body, that it may be fashioned like unto his glorious body...." (Philippians 3:20-21).

Understanding the hope of His calling provides both the motivation and faith to begin, increasingly, in advance of heaven, to realize this glorious prospect in our lives here below, for "...every man that hath this hope in him purifieth himself, even as he is pure" (1 John 3:3). Paul said it like this: "Set your affection on things above, not on things on the earth. For ye are dead, and your life is hid with Christ in God. When Christ, who is our life shall appear, then shall ye also appear with him in glory. Mortify therefore your members which are upon the earth..." (Colossians 3:2-5).

This glorious calling for both Jew and Gentile to become the children of God and to dwell eternally in heaven was unknown to Old Testament saints. Paul called it "the mystery which hath been hid from ages and from generations...which is Christ in you, the hope of glory." His passion was to "present every man perfect in Christ Jesus..." (Colossians 1:26-28). That heavenly perfection will be fully realized only at the Rapture: "Beloved, now are we the sons of God, and...when he shall appear, we shall be like him; for we shall see him as he is" (1 John 3:2). What a hope, to be like Him eternally!

In the meantime, we are to become more and more like our Lord as "we all, with open face, beholding as in a glass the glory of the Lord, are changed into the same image from glory to glory, even as by the Spirit of the Lord" (2 Corinthians 3:18). Recognizing our failure to glorify Him as we should in our bodies and spirits, which are His (1 Corinthians 6:20), we long not so much for crowns or rewards but *to be like Him*.

Surely Paul said it for all of us: "...this one thing I do, forgetting those things which are behind, and reaching forth unto those things which are before, I press toward the mark for the prize of the high calling of God in Christ Jesus" (Philippians 3:13-14). It is not enough to look forward with eager anticipation to that day when we shall see Christ and be fully like Him. We are here and now to "press toward the mark for the prize" of this high calling—for ourselves and for others as well. Concerning this "hope of glory," Paul declared, "Whereunto I also labor, striving according to his working, which worketh in me mightily" (Colossians 1:29).

Always there must be that balance between the working of God's miraculous power in and through us and our working together with Him: "...work out [not for] your own salvation with fear and trembling. For it is God which worketh in you both to will and to do of his good pleasure" (Philippians

2:12-13). Paul gave everything he had to be and do all that God intended for him: "I follow after [to] apprehend that for which also I am apprehended of Christ Jesus..." (3:12).

When bygone failures would haunt us, God's solution is clear: "forgetting those things which are behind...press toward... the high calling...." We do not dwell on the past, nourishing the regrets that would imprison us. All is under the blood of Christ; and we dishonor Him by continuing to be burdened with that which He has forgiven and forgotten.

Our joy is in the future prospect of realizing the hope of His calling, of being forever with Him and like Him in His eternal glory. A foretaste of that glory can be realized here below in ever greater measure through Christ dwelling in our hearts by faith (Ephesians 3:17). May the hope of His calling grip us and propel us onward and upward in fulfilling His will here below as we await His coming!

The Berean Call, May, 2001

(RE)SET YOUR AFFECTION

IN VARIOUS BOOKS and articles through the years, we have discussed the kingdom/dominion/reconstruction/COR movement a number of times. This writer considers it to be the fastest growing adverse influence in the church today, and thus a primary cause for concern. It is helping to set the stage for the coming world government of the Antichrist by confusing key issues of prophecy. Of course, those involved in this movement would sincerely deny that they are helping, or that they wish to have any part in helping, the Antichrist in any way. There is another and more subtle danger—the undermining of one's personal spiritual life as a result of this movement's unbiblical teachings.

Those who believe that they must take over the world and establish the millennial kingdom for Christ in His absence either reject the Rapture or relegate it to such a distant and unimportant position that it has no practical value in their lives. This has serious consequences because the hope that Christ could return at any moment is intended by God to be one of the major purifying factors in the Christian's life (1 John 3:3). I believe that John is referring both to doctrinal as well as moral purity by the phrase "purifieth himself." The two go together, yet doctrine is now frequently avoided as a cause of division rather than what it actually is, the necessary container of truth.

One of the most unpopular doctrines today (in stark contrast to its prominence only a few years ago) is that of the Rapture—Christ catching His bride away to heaven (1 Thessalonians 4:13-18). Because Christ has not come "quickly," as He promised (at least by our definition), there are those who consider the Rapture a topic to be avoided. However, the great number of statements in the Bible regarding the end times in general, and the Rapture in particular, suggest that this whole area should be a prominent part of our Christian faith and life.

With respect to the Rapture, we are repeatedly urged to have an attitude of *watching and waiting*. Why is this attitude commanded by Christ? Does its value for us, and the importance the Bible obviously attaches to it, reside primarily in the Lord's return actually being imminent? Indeed not.

Whether or not the Lord's return is imminent for *us*, we now know in retrospect that it was not imminent for all those generations of Christians who came before us. If the sole value of their "expectancy" lay in its being satisfied, i.e., in it being *true* that the Lord would come imminently—then the fact that Christ has not yet returned would leave us without any explanation for why the Lord urged this "expectant" attitude in the first place. Therefore there must be something important, something integral to a good Christian life, about the attitude of expecting Christ's return at any moment. What could this be?

There can be no doubt that believing that we could be caught up at any moment imparts an added seriousness to our lives. We won't be here forever, so we should make every minute count. Moreover, it makes us insecure in our tendency to identify ourselves too closely with a world which does not hold our ultimate destiny, and reminds us of our true citizenship in a world to come which is based upon eternal rather than earthly values. This attitude certainly ought to characterize a Christian life, and a lively sense of the possibility of Christ's imminent return is more than justified if it has this good effect on us.

But doesn't the possibility of imminent death supply exactly the same motive? No. While it supplies a very powerful motive indeed, there is a great difference. The expectancy of being caught up at any moment into the presence of our Lord in the Rapture does have some advantages over a similar expectancy through the possibility of sudden death:

First: If we are in a right relationship with Christ, we can genuinely *look forward* to the Rapture. Yet no one (not even Christ in the Garden) looks forward to death. The joyful prospect of the Rapture will attract our thoughts, while the distasteful prospect of death is something we may try to forget about, thus making it less effective in our daily lives.

Second: While the Rapture is similar to death in that both serve to end one's earthly life, the Rapture does something else as well: it signals the climax of history and opens the curtain upon its final drama. It thus ends, in a way that death does not, all human stake in continuing earthly developments, such as the lives of the children left behind, the growth or dispersion of the fortune accumulated, the protection of one's personal repu-tation, the success of whatever earthly causes one has espoused, and so forth.

One way that people cope with the finality of death is through such forms of pseudo-immortality—ways in which we, or things we cared about, "live on" after we are gone. Even Christians, who have genuine immortality to look forward to, may nevertheless be tempted to find consolation in some of these forms of pseudo-immortality. The Rapture, however, undercuts all of these; and to whatever extent these pseudo-consolations are weakened, our post-mortem hope becomes purified of its earthly elements. Being thus forced to face the fact that our destiny lies in heaven, we will be motivated to live with that goal in mind.

Third: The incentive provided by death is weakened some-what by the fact that we generally have at least some control over its relative imminence. Certainly we are radically contin-gent beings, and our lives could be snuffed out at any time. But this is not the way people usually die. The cancer victim could have refrained from smoking, or added more fiber to his diet, or sought treatment earlier. The guilty auto accident victim could have driven within the speed limit or taken a taxi when he had too much to drink.

Though death can come suddenly and without warning we are not complete masters of our own fate), it is nevertheless true that we make decisions daily that increase or decrease the chances of our dying tomorrow, next month, or in ten years. This not-altogether-illusory sense of control over the time of our death reduces its incentive for godliness by making us feel that we can afford to postpone a closer relationship with

God until next week, next month or next year. In contrast, we have absolutely no control over the timing of Christ's return to earth. It will just happen "out of the blue." Belief in the imminent return of Christ, then, does not allow us to postpone anything.

The whole dominion/reconstruction movement is too wedded to an ongoing earthly process stretching into the indeterminate future to be truly faithful to the totality of what Scripture says about being sufficiently disengaged from this world to be ready to leave it behind at a moment's notice. I am concerned that the Reconstructionists and the Coalition on Revival as well as other kingdom/dominion advocates are fostering a false conception of our earthly ministry—a conception which we must guard against lest we subtly fall into an attitude like that of Dostoevsky's Grand Inquisitor, for whom Christ's return to earth represents an interference with the mission of the church. He has Christ thrown into prison, where he visits him to complain:

> There is no need for Thee to come now at all. Thou must not meddle for the time, at least...fortunately, departing Thou didst hand on the work to us. Thou has promised, Thou hast established by Thy word, Thou has given to us the right to bind and to unbind, and now, of course, Thou canst not think of taking it away. Why, then, hast Thou come to hinder us?

All human beings are tempted to be more at home in the world than they should be. Christians are not exempt from this temptation, and when they succumb it often leads to an effort to reinterpret Scripture accordingly. Reconstructionists exemplify this temptation, some even taking it to the point of claiming that Christ returned in A.D.70 in the person of the Roman armies to destroy Jerusalem and excommunicate Israel—and that this was the day of the church's wedding to Christ prophesied in Revelation 19!

Christ's return before they have taken over the world would be as inconvenient to the Reconstructionists and others in the kingdom/dominion movement as it was to the Grand Inquisitor, and for the same reasons.

Our hope is not in taking over this world, but in being taken to heaven by our Lord, to be married to Him in glory and then to return with Him as part of the armies of heaven to rescue Israel, destroy His enemies and participate in His millennial reign. Yet too often those of us who claim to believe this hold the belief in theory only, while denying it with our lives. Our hearts should be in perpetual wonder and joy at the prospect of being suddenly caught up to be with Christ, our bodies transformed to be like His body of glory and to be wedded to our Lord for eternity.

Heaven is not so much a location *somewhere* as it is being with Christ *wherever* He may be in the universe at the time, for we will be perpetually in His presence. It is not so much a *place* as it is a *state of being*, enjoying a heavenly existence that is beyond our present understanding but which ought to be our continual and exciting anticipation. And in our transformed bodies, made like His body of glory, in which we will share His resurrection life, we will reign with Him over this earth for 1,000 years. Then we will spend an eternity during which He will be perpetually revealing to and in us more and more of Himself, His love and grace and kindness.

Part of the problem with the kingdom/dominion/recon-struction movement is its mistaken notion that mortal man can accomplish what only immortal Man, our risen Lord, and we as immortal resurrected beings with Him, can perform. Do not settle for anything less than the fullness of what Christ has promised! The glory of the eternal kingdom that He offers is light years beyond the COR agenda of Christianizing and taking over this present world in these bodies of weakness and corruption.

We can miss His best by refusing to take seriously what the Bible clearly teaches and by not standing firm for sound doctrine. And we can also miss out on our true reward by attempting to live in our own strength the Christian life which only Christ can live through us. May we be true to His Word and to Him in our daily lives. The joy and glory He has planned and in which He desires that we participate is more than enough to excite and inspire and motivate us. "Set your affection on things above" (Colossians 3:2)!

Originally titled "Imminence"
The Berean Call, *October, 1988*

Jesus answered, My kingdom is not of this world:
if my kingdom were of this world, then would
my servants fight, that I should not be delivered to the
Jews: but now is my kingdom not from hence.

—JOHN 18:36

In my Father's house are many mansions: if it were not
so, I would have told you. I go to prepare a place for
you. And if I go and prepare a place for you, I will come
again, and receive you unto myself; that where I am,
there ye may be also.

—JOHN 14:2-3

But the day of the Lord will come as a thief in the
night; in the which the heavens shall pass away with
a great noise, and the elements shall melt with fervent
heat, the earth also and the works that are therein
shall be burned up. . . . Nevertheless we, according to
his promise, look for new heavens and a new earth,
wherein dwelleth righteousness.

—2 PETER 3:10, 13

ENDNOTES

Foreword

1. R. W. Southern, *Western Society and the Church in the Middle Ages* (Penguin Books, Vol. 2 of *Pelican History of the Church Series*, 1970), 18-19, cited in Dave Hunt, *Whatever Happened to Heaven?* (Harvest House, 1988), 150-51.

2. Will Durant, *The Reformation: A History of European Civilizations from Wyclif to Calvin: 1300-1564* (Simon & Schuster, 1957), 472-73, cited in Hunt, *Heaven* , 175-76.

3. Edwin Muir, *John Knox: Portrait of a Calvinist* (The Viking Press, 1929), 106-8, cited in Hunt, *Heaven*, 174-75.

4. Hunt, *Heaven*, 174.

5. Ern Baxter (associate of William Branham), cited in Sandy Simpson, "Dominionism Exposed," http://www.deceptioninthechurch.com /dominionismexposed.html.

6. Gary North, *Christian Reconstructionism: The Attack on the "New" Pentecostal*, January/February 1988, Vol. X, No. 1.

Chapter 1

1. William J. Bouwsma, *John Calvin: A Sixteenth Century Portrait* (United Kingdom: Oxford University Press, 1988), 10.

2. Will Durant, "The Reformation," Pt. VI of *The Story of Civilization* (New York: Simon and Schuster, 1957), 460.

3. Loraine Boettner, *The Reformed Doctrine of Predestination* (Philipsburg, NJ: Presbyterian and Reformed Publishing Co., 1932), 403.

4. John Calvin, "Method and Arrangement," in *Institutes of the Christian Religion*, trans. Henry Beveridge (Grand Rapids, MI: Wm. Eerdmans Publishing Company, 1998 ed.), IV: xv, 3.

5. Ibid., 1–6; xvi, 24, etc.

6. Roland Bainton, *Michel Servet, heretique et martyr* (Geneva: Iroz 1953), 152-153, quoting letter of February 26, 1533, now lost.

7. Bernard Cottret, *Calvin: A Biography* (Grand Rapids, MI: William B. Eerdmans, 2000), 129; Calvin, *Institutes*, IV: xv, 16; IV: xvi, 31.

8. John Calvin, *Commentary on Psalms—Volume 1*, Author's Preface, www.cal.org/c/calvin/comment3/comm_vol08/htm/TOC.htm.

9. J. D. Douglas, *Who's Who In Christian History*, 128–29; cited in Henry R. Pike, *The Other Side of John Calvin* (Head to Heart, n. d.), 9–10. See also Alister E. McGrath, *A Life of John Calvin* (Cambridge, MA: Blackwell Publishers, 1990), 73; and Jones, *Reformation.*, 127.

10. R. Tudor Jones, *The Great Reformation* (Downer's Grove, IL: InterVarsity Press, n. d.), 127.

11. Calvin, *Commentary on Psalms*, Preface.

12. Durant, "Reformation," VI: *Civilization*, 459–60.

13. Calvin, *Institutes*, I:vii,4.

14. Ibid., viii,1.

15. Leonard Verduin, *The Reformers and Their Stepchildren* (Sarasota, FL: Christian Hymnary Publishers, 1991), 66.

16. Augustine, *On the Gift of Perseverance*, chapter 47, http://whitefield.freeservices.com/augustine06.html.

17. R. C. Sproul, *Grace Unknown* (Grand Rapids, MI: Baker Books, 1997), 189.

18. Calvin, *Institutes*, III: xxiii, 6.

19. R. C. Sproul, Jr., *Almighty Over All* (Grand Rapids, MI: Baker Books, 1999), 54.

20. Calvin, *Institutes*, III: xxiii, 1.

21. Ibid., 3.

22. Ibid., 4.

23. Ibid., 6.

24. Ibid., 10-11.

25. Ibid., xxi–xxii.

26. Ibid., xxi, 7.

27. Ibid., II: v, 19.

28. Canons of Dort (Dordrecht, Holland, 1619), 1,6.

29. Calvin, *Institutes*, III: xxi, 1.

30. Ibid., II: xii, 5.

31. Ibid., III: xxiii, 2,4.

32. C. H. Spurgeon, *Metropolitan Tabernacle Pulpit*, Vol. 26:49–52.

Chapter 2

1. David N. Steele and Curtis C. Thomas, *The Five Points of Calvinism* (Phillipsburg, NJ: Presbyterian and Reformed Publishing Co., 1963), 19.

2. Laurence M. Vance, *The Other Side of Calvinism* (Pensacola, FL: Vance Publications, rev. ed., 1999), 37.

3. Kenneth G. Talbot and W. Gary Crampton, *Calvinism, Hyper-Calvinism and Arminianism* (Edmonton, AB: Still Water Revival Books, 1990), 78.

4. Benjamin B. Warfield, *Calvin and Augustine*, ed. Samuel G. Craig (Phillipsburg, NJ: Presbyterian and Reformed Publishing Co., 1956), 22.

5. John Piper, *The Legacy of Sovereign Joy: God's Triumphant Grace in the Lives of Augustine, Luther, and Calvin* (Wheaton, IL: Crossway Books, 2000), 24-25.

6. Charles Haddon Spurgeon, ed., *Exposition of the Doctrine of Grace* (Pasadena, CA: Pilgrim Publications, n. d.), 298.

7. Alvin L. Baker, *Berkouwer's Doctrine of Election: Balance or Imbalance?* (Phillipsburg, NJ: Presbyterian and Reformed Publishing Co., 1981), 25.

8. St. Augustine, *A Treatment On the Soul and its Origins*, Book IV, 16.

9. C. Gregg Singer, *John Calvin: His Roots and Fruits* (Abingdon Press, 1989), vii.

10. Vance, *Other Side*, 40.

11. John Calvin, "A Treatise on the Eternal Predestination of God," in *John Calvin, Calvin's Calvinism*, trans. Henry Cole (Grandville, MI: Reformed Free Publishing Association, 1987), 38; cited in Vance, *Other Side*, 38.

12. Leonard Verduin, *The Reformers and Their Stepchildren* (Sarasota, FL: Christian Hymnary Publishers, 1991), 33.

13. Petilian II.85.189; cited in W. H. C. Frend, *The Rise of Christianity* (Philadelphia, PA: Fortress Press, 1984), 671.

14. Frend, *Rise*, 671.

15. Ibid., 672.

16. F.F. Bruce, *Light in the West,* Bk. III of *The Spreading Flame* (Grand Rapids, MI: Wm. B. Eerdmans Publishing Co, 1956), 60-61.

17. E. H. Broadbent, *The Pilgrim Church* (Port Colborne, ON: Gospel Folio Press, reprint 1999), 49.

18. Henry H. Milman, *History of Christianity* (New York: A. C. Armstrong and Son, 1886), 3:176.

19. Warfield, Calvin, v.

20. John Calvin, contents page of *Institutes of the Christian Religion*, trans. Henry Beveridge (Grand Rapids, MI: Wm. B. Eerdmans Publishing Co., 1998 ed.), III: xxiii, IV: xvii, etc.

21. Calvin, *Institutes*, III: xxi, 2.

22. Ibid., xxi, 4.

23. Ibid., xxiii, 1.

24. Ibid., 5.

25. Ibid.

26. Ibid., 8.

27. Ibid., IV: xiii, 9.

28. Ibid., III: xxiii, 11.

29. Ibid., 13.

30. Ibid., 14.

31. Richard A. Muller, *Christ and the Decree* (Grand Rapids, MI: Baker Book House, 1988), 22.

32. Norman L. Geisler, *What Augustine Says* (Grand Rapids, MI: Baker Book House, 1982), 9.

33. Aug. Cont. Epist. Fundament c.v.

34. John Paul II, Sovereign Pontiff, *Augustineum Hyponensem* (Apostolic Letter, August 28, 1986. Available at: www. cin.org/jp2.ency/augustin .html).

35. Dave Hunt and James White, *Debating Calvinism*, (Sisters, OR: Multnomah Publishers, 2004), 244.

36. Calvin, *Institutes*, I: vii, 3.

37. Talbot and Crampton, *Calvinism, Hyper-Calvinism*, 78; cited in Vance, Other Side, 39.

38. Alexander Souter, *The Earliest Latin Commentaries on the Epistles of St. Paul* (n. p., 1927), 139.

39. N. L. Rice, *God Sovereign and Man Free* (Harrisonburg, VA: Sprinkle Publications, 1985), 13.

40. Benjamin B. Warfield, "The Idea of Systematic Theology," in *The Princeton Theology*, ed. Mark A. Noll (Phillipsburg, NJ: Presbyterian and Reformed Publishing Co., 1983), 258.

41. Vance, *Other Side*, 41.

42. Richard N. Ostling, "The Second Founder of the Faith" (*Time*, September 29, 1986).

43. William P. Grady, *Final Authority: A Christian's Guide to the King James Bible* (Knoxville, TN: Grady Publications, 1993), 54.

44. Sir Robert Anderson, *The Bible or the Church?* (London: Pickering and Inglis, 2nd ed., n. d.), 53.

45. Augustine, *The City of God*, trans. Marcus Dods. In *Great Books of the Western World*, ed. Robert Maynard Hutchins and Mortimer J. Adler (Encyclopaedia Brittanica, Inc., 1952), XX:7, 8.

46. Vance, *Other Side*, 55.

47. Talbot and Crampton, *Calvinism, Hyper-Calvinism*, 79.

48. Calvin, *Institutes*, IV:xiv, 26.

49. Alister E. McGrath, *The Life of John Calvin* (Cambridge, MA: Blackwell Publishers, 1990), 151.

50. Francois Wendel, *Calvin: Origins and Development of His Religious Thought* (Grand Rapids, MI: Baker Books, 1997), 124.

51. Vance, *Other Side*; citing Calvin, *Institutes*, 139, 146, 148–49.

52. Vance, *Other Side*, 113; citing Wendel, *Origins*, 264, and Timothy George, *Theology of the Reformers* (Nashville, TN: Broadman Press, 1988), 232.

53. Philip Schaff, *History of the Christian Church* (New York: Charles Scribner's Sons, 1910; Grand Rapids, MI: Wm B. Eerdmans Publishing Co., reprint 1959), III: 1018.

54. Warfield, *Calvin*, 322.

55. Ibid., 313.

56. Ibid., 318.

57. Philip F. Congdon, "Soteriological Implications of Five-point Calvinism," *Journal of the Grace Evangelical Society*, Autumn 1995, 8:15, 55–68.

58. George, *Theology*, 68.

59. James R. White to Dave Hunt, August 4, 2000. On file.

60. David Schaff, *Our Father's Faith and Ours*, 172; cited in Samuel Fisk, *Calvinistic Paths Retraced* (Raleigh, NC: Biblical Evangelism Press, 1985), 68.

61. Philip Schaff, *History*, II:975–76.

62. Samuel Fisk, *Calvinistic Paths Retraced* (Raleigh, NC: Biblical Evangelism Press, 1985), 68.

63. Grady, *Final Authority*, 35.

64. Fisk, *Calvinistic*, 67.

65. F. F. Bruce, *The Books and the Parchments* (London: Pickering and Inglis, Ltd., 1950), 191.

66. Bruce, *Books*, 194–95.

67. Merrill F. Unger, *Unger's Bible Dictionary* (Chicago, IL: Moody Press, 1969), 1151–54.

68. Fisk, *Calvinistic*, 70–75.

69. F.F. Bruce, *The English Bible: A History of Translations* (New York: Oxford University Press, 1961), 90-91.

70. Charles C. Butterworth, *The Literary Lineage of the King James Bible* (Philadelphia: University of Pennsylvania Press, 1941), 163.

71. H. Wheeler Robinson, *The Bible In Its Ancient and English Versions* (Oxford: Clarendon Press, 1940), 186, 206–207.

72. Loraine Boettner, *The Reformed Doctrine of Predestination* (Phillipsburg, NJ : Presbyterian and Reformed Publishing Co., 1932), 405.

73. Spurgeon, *Exposition*, 298; cited in Vance, *Other Side*, 38.

Chapter 3

1. W. H. C. Frend, *The Rise of Christianity* (Philadelphia, PA: Fortress Press, 1984), 482.

2. Philip Schaff, *History of the Christian Church* (New York: Charles Scribner's Sons, 1910; Wm. B. Eerdmans Publishing Company, reprint 1959), II:72–73.

3. Ibid.

4. F. F. Bruce, *Light in the West*, Bk. III of *The Spreading Flame* (Grand Rapids, MI: Wm B. Eerdmans Publishing Co., 1956), 11–13.

5. *Codex Theodosianus*, (July 3, A.D. 321), XVI:8.1.

6. Frend, *Rise*, 484.

7. Will Durant, "Caesar and Christ," Pt. III of *The Story of Civilization* (New York: Simon and Schuster, 1950), 656.

8. Philip Hughes, *A History of the Church* (London, 1934), 1:198.

9. E. H. Broadbent, *The Pilgrim Church* (Port Colborne, ON: Gospel Folio Press, reprint 1999), 38–39.

10. Frend, *Rise*, 492.

11. John Laurence Mosheim, *An Ecclesiastical History, Ancient and Modern*, trans. Archibald MacLaine (Cincinnati: Applegate and Co., 1854), 101; and many other historians.

12. Laurence M. Vance, *The Other Side of Calvinism* (Pensacola, FL: Vance Publications, rev. ed. 1999), 45.

13. Edward Gibbon, *The History of the Decline and Fall of the Roman Empire* (New York: Modern Library, n. d.), 2:233.

14. John W. Kennedy, *The Torch of the Testimony* (Christian Books Publishing House, 1963), 68.

15. John Calvin, *Institutes of the Christian Religion*, trans. Henry Beveridge (Grand Rapids, MI: Wm. B. Eerdmans Publishing Company, 1998 ed.), III: xxv, 5.

16. Bernard Cottret, *Calvin: A Biography*, trans. M. Wallace McDonald (Grand Rapids, MI: William B. Eerdmans Publishing Company, 2000), 128-130.

17. Loraine Boettner, *The Reformed Doctrine of Predestination* (Phillipsburg, NJ: Presbyterian and Reformed Publishing Co., 1932), 408.

18. Stefan Zweig, Eden Paul and Cedar Paul, trans., *The Right to Heresy* (London: Cassell and Company, 1936), 57; cited in Henry R. Pike, *The Other Side of John Calvin* (Head to Heart, n. d.), 21–22.

19. Francois Wendel, *Calvin: Origins and Development of His Religious Thought* (Grand Rapids, MI: Baker Books, 1997), 98-101; Cottret, *Calvin*, 195-198.

20. Wendel, *Calvin*, 100; Cottret, *Calvin*, 198-200.

21. Cottret, *Calvin*, 200.

22. Roget Amédée, *L'Église et l'État a Genève du temps de Calvin. Étude d'histoire politico-ecclésiastique* (Geneva: J. Jullien, 1867).

23. Bernard Cottret, *Calvin: A Biography*, tr. M. Wallace McDonald (Grand Rapids, MI: William B. Eerdmans Publishing Company, 2000) 250.

24. Durant, *Civilization*, III: 474.

25. George Park Fisher, *The Reformation* (New York: Scribner, Armstrong and Co., 1873), 224.

26. Boettner, *Reformed*, 410.

27. Ronald S. Wallace, *Calvin, Geneva, and the Reformation* (Grand Rapids, MI: Baker Book House, 1990), 29.

28. Calvin, *Institutes*, IV: xx, 2.

29. Ibid., 3.

30. Zweig, *Erasmus*, 217.

31. Pike, *John Calvin*, 26.

32. John T. McNeil, *The History and Character of Calvinism* (Oxford: Oxford University Press, 1966), 189.

33. Williston Walker, John Calvin: *The Organizer of Reformed Protestantism* (New York: Schocken Books, 1969), 259.

34. Ibid., 107.

35. Schaff, *History*, 8:357.

36. Durant, *Civilization*, VI: 473.

37. Vance, *Other Side*, 85.

38. Durant, *Civilization*, IV: 465.

39. Frend, *Rise*, 669.

40. *The Register of the Company of Pastors of Geneva in the Time of Calvin,* trans. and ed. Philip E. Hughes (Grand Rapids, MI: Wm B. Eerdmans Publishing Co., 1966), 137–38; cited in Vance, *Other Side*, 84.

41. Schaff, *History*, 8:618.

42. G. R. Potter and M. Greengrass, *John Calvin* (New York: St. Martin's Press, 1983), 92–93.

43. *Register of Geneva*, cited in Vance, *Other Side*, 201.

44. Schaff, *History*, 502.

45. Fisher, *Reformation*, 222.

46. J. M. Robertson, *Short History of Freethought* (London, 1914), I:443–44.

47. Cottret, *Biography*, 180-181.

48. Ibid.

49. Wendel, *Calvin*, 85.

50. Schaff, *History*, 644.

51. Bard Thompson, *Humanists and Reformers: A History of the Renaissance and Reformation* (Grand Rapids, MI: Wm B. Eerdmans Publishing Co., 1996), 501.

52. Schaff, *History*, 519.

53. C. Gregg Singer, *John Calvin: His Roots and Fruits* (Abingdon Press, 1989), 19.

54. Otto Scott, *The Great Christian Revolution* (Windsor, NY: The Reformer Library, 1994), 46.

55. Charles Beard, *The Reformation of the Sixteenth Century in Relation to Modern Thought and Knowledge* (London, 1885), 353; also see Edwin Muir, *John Knox* (London, 1920), 108.

56. Preserved Smith, *The Age of the Reformation* (New York, 1920), 174.

57. James R. White, *The Potter's Freedom* (Amityville, NY: Calvary Press Publishing, 2000), 98.

58. R. C. Sproul, *Chosen by God* (Carol Stream, IL: Tyndale House Publishers, Inc., 1986), 72.

59. Durant, *Civilization*, VI:481.

60. Roland Bainton, *Hunted Heretic: The Life of Michael Servetus* (Boston: The Beacon Press, 1953), 144; cited in Durant, *Civilization*, VI:481. See also John Calvin, *The Letters of John Calvin* (Carlisle, PA: The Banner of Truth Trust, 1980), 159.

61. John Calvin, dated August 20, 1553; quoted in Calvin, *Letters*.

62. Wallace, *Calvin, Geneva*, 77.

63. Durant, *Civilization*, VI: 483.

64. Ibid., 484.

65. Cottret, *Biography*, 78.

66. Calvin, *Institutes*, IV: xvi, 31.

67. Frend, *Rise*, 672.

68. Frederic W. Farrar, *History of Interpretation* (New York: E. P. Dutton and Co., 1886), 235–38.

69. Ferdinand Buisson, Sebastien Castellion. *Sa Vie et son oeuvre* (1515-1563) (Paris: Hachette, 1892), I:354.

70. Letter from N. Zurkinden to Calvin, February 10, 1554, cited in Cottret, 227.

71. J. W. Allen, *History of Political Thought in the Sixteenth Century* (London, 1951), 87.

72. R. Tudor Jones, *The Great Reformation* (Downer's Grove, IL: InterVarsity Press, n. d.), 140.

73. John Calvin to the Marquis de Poet, in *The Works of Voltaire* (Chicago: E. R. Dumont, 1901), 4:89; quoted in Vance, *Other Side*, 95, who gives two other sources for this quote.

74. Schaff, *History*, 8:690–91.

75. William Cunningham, *The Reformers and the Theology of the Reformation* (Carlisle, PA: The Banner of Truth Trust, 1967), 316–17.

76. Scott, *Revolution*, 100.

77. Singer, *Roots*, 32.

78. William Jones, *The History of the Christian Church* (Church History Research and Archives, 5th ed. 1983), 2:238.

Chapter 4

1. John Calvin, *Acts of the Council of Trent: With the Antidote*, ed. and trans. Henry Beveridge (1851); in *Selected Works of John Calvin: Tracts and Letters*, 7 vols., ed. Henry Beveridge and Jules Bonnet (Grand Rapids, MI: Baker Books, 1983), 3:111.

2. James R. White, *The Potter's Freedom* (Amityville, NY: Calvary Press Publishing, 2000), 247.

3. Arthur W. Pink, *The Sovereignty of God* (Grand Rapids, MI: Baker Book House, 2nd prtg. 1986), 12.

4. Pink, *Sovereignty*, 144.

5. David J. Engelsma, *Hyper-Calvinism and the Call of the Gospel* (Grandville, MI: Reformed Free Publishing Association, 1980), 53.

6. Paul K. Jewett, *Election and Predestination* (Grand Rapids, MI: Wm B. Eerdmans Publishing Co., 1985 ed.), 3–4.

7. John Piper, *The Justification of God: An Exegetical and Theological Study of Romans 9:1–23* (Grand Rapids, MI: Baker Books, 2000), 179.

8. J. I. Packer, "The Love of God: Universal and Particular," in *Still Sovereign,* ed. Thomas R. Schreiner and Bruce A. Ware (Grand Rapids, MI: Baker Books, 2000), 283–84.

9. Edwin H. Palmer, *the five points of calvinism* (Grand Rapids, MI: Baker Books, enlarged ed., 20th prtg. 1999), 95, 124–25.

10. White, *Potter's*, 137.

11. Piper, *Justification*, 82–83.

12. John Piper and Pastoral Staff, "TULIP: What We Believe about the Five Points of Calvinism: Position Paper of the Pastoral Staff" (Minneapolis, MN: Desiring God Ministries, 1997), 3.

13. John Piper, *The Legacy of Sovereign Joy: God's Triumphant Grace in the Lives of Augustine, Luther, and Calvin* (Wheaton, IL: Crossway Books, 2000), 18.

14. Ibid., 38.

15. Ibid., 24–25.

16. Ibid., 32–35.

17. Ibid., 34–38.

OTHER BOOKS BY DAVE HUNT

THE SEDUCTION OF CHRISTIANITY:
SPIRITUAL DISCERNMENT IN THE LAST DAYS
—*Dave Hunt & T. A. McMahon*

The Bible clearly states that a great Apostasy must occur before Christ's Second Coming. Today Christians are being deceived by a worldview that is more subtle and more seductive than anything ever before experienced. As delusions and deceptions continue to grow, this book will guide you in the truth of God's Word. Harvest House, 239 pages.

ISBN: 0-89081-441-4 • TBC: B04414

WHATEVER HAPPENED TO HEAVEN? —*Dave Hunt*

Today, a growing number of Christians are exchanging the hope of the Rapture for a "new" hope: that Christians can clean up society and elect enough of their own candidates to political office to make this world a "heaven on earth." In this timeless (and timely!) reprint of his 1988 bestseller, Dave provides an easily understood explanation of the popular "divisive" issues and with fascinating clarity spurs readers toward restored faith in our blessed hope. The Berean Call, 327 pages.

ISBN: 978-1-928660-70-5 • TBC: B60705

AMERICA, THE SORCERER'S NEW APPRENTICE:
THE RISE OF NEW AGE SHAMANISM —*Dave Hunt & T.A. McMahon*

Americans are rapidly "awakening" to what is being hailed as a paradigm shift in global consciousness—which many equate to a spiritual "rebirth" of humanity in light of ancient prophecies surrounding the year 2012. This fascinating reprint of the classic 1988 volume will astound you with groundbreaking revelations and prophetic implications. The Berean Call, 294 pages.

ISBN: 978-1-928660-69-9 • TBC: B60699

Other Books by Dave Hunt

GLOBAL PEACE AND THE RISE OF ANTICHRIST —*Dave Hunt*

Many are calling this 1990 classic "a book ahead of its time." Have things changed in two decades? The Bible declares that one-world government and a universally accepted "new" spirituality are coming. Although some of the players on the global stage have changed, Satan's stratagems remain the same. Readers will gain valuable insight for today—and tomorrow—from this riveting historic and prophetic perspective. The Berean Call, 321 pages.

ISBN: 978-1-928660-68-2 • TBC: B60682

IN DEFENSE OF THE FAITH: BIBLICAL ANSWERS TO CHALLENGING QUESTIONS —*Dave Hunt*

Why does God allow suffering and evil? What about all the "contradictions" in the Bible? Are some people predestined to go to hell? This book tackles the tough issues, including why a merciful God would punish people who have never heard of Christ, and how to tell the difference between God's workings and Satan's. Harvest House, 373 pages.

ISBN: 978-1-928660-66-8 • TBC: B60668

COUNTDOWN TO THE SECOND COMING: A CHRONOLOGY OF PROPHETIC EARTH EVENTS HAPPENING NOW —*Dave Hunt*

At last, a book that presents in a concise manner the events leading up to the return of Christ. Dave Hunt, in his characteristic direct style, answers questions such as, Who is the Antichrist? How will he be recognized? How are current events indicators that we really are in the last of the last days? The Berean Call, 95 pages.

ISBN: 1-928660-19-3 • TBC: B00193

WHAT LOVE IS THIS?
CALVINISM'S MISREPRESENTATION OF GOD —*Dave Hunt*

Multitudes who believe they understand Calvinism will be shocked to discover its Roman Catholic roots and Calvin's grossly unchristian behavior as the "Protestant Pope" of Geneva, Switzerland. It is our prayer that this book will enable readers to examine more carefully the vital issues involved and to follow God's Holy Word and not man. The Berean Call, 590 pages.

ISBN: 1-928660-12-6 • TBC: B03000

SEEKING & FINDING GOD:
IN SEARCH OF THE TRUE FAITH —*Dave Hunt*

Surprisingly, consumers examine the quality and calories of a food item with more care than they consider their eternal destiny. With compelling proofs, this book demonstrates that the issue of where one will spend eternity is not a matter of preference. In fact, there is overwhelming evidence that we are eternal beings who will spend eternity somewhere. But where will it be? And how can we know? The Berean Call, 159 pages.

ISBN:1-928660-23-1 • TBC: B04425

JUDGMENT DAY!
ISLAM, ISRAEL, AND THE NATIONS —*Dave Hunt*

In what is possibly the most comprehensive and clear-cut examination of ancient biblical prophecy and Middle East politics, *Judgment Day!* reveals the ancient agenda against the Jews, and traces its twisted trail to modern deceptions by U.S. Presidents, foreign ambassadors, military leaders, businesspeople, educators, and world leaders alike. Skillfully dissecting fraudulent Palestinian claims to "the Promised Land," this page-turner exposes the fraud, deceit, and treachery of an international community allied against the Jewish nation. The Berean Call, 455 pages.

ISBN: 1-928660-32-3 • TBC: B05858

YOGA AND THE BODY OF CHRIST:
WHAT POSITION SHOULD CHRISTIANS HOLD? —*Dave Hunt*

Yoga is rapidly revolutionizing the fitness industry worldwide—and is even extending its reach directly into the churches and lifestyles of professing Christians. But is it "simply stretching" as some believers claim? Or is there serious danger in this Hindu practice, designed to awaken Kundalini energy (which, literally defined, means "Serpent Power"? The Berean Call, 175 pages.

ISBN: 978-1-928660-48-4 • TBC: B60487

PSYCHOLOGY AND THE CHURCH:
CRITICAL QUESTIONS, CRUCIAL ANSWERS
—Dave Hunt & T. A. McMahon

While prominent Christian pastors and leaders embrace psychotherapy, acclaimed secular psychologists acknowledge that it is, in fact, a religious practice under the guise of medical science. If true, why have so many evangelicals blindly adopted psychotherapy? And how did the early Christians manage to cope without it for nearly 2000 years? The Berean Call, 413 pages.

ISBN: 1-928660-61-3 • TBC: B60613

COSMOS, CREATOR, AND HUMAN DESTINY:
ANSWERING DARWIN, DAWKINS, AND THE NEW ATHEISTS
—Dave Hunt

This explosive book is more than enough to demolish the strongholds of both cosmic and secular humanists alike. The author explores the fascinating reaches of our fragile human existence in the magnificent yet mysterious space-time continuum, covering territory that Charles Darwin failed to address and where even Richard Dawkins fears to tread. The Berean Call, 606 pages.

ISBN: 978-1-928660-64-4 • TBC: B60644

TULIP AND THE BIBLE:
COMPARING THE WORKS OF CALVIN WITH THE WORD OF GOD

—by Dave Hunt

SELECTED MATERIAL FROM THE BESTSELLING HARDCOVER, WHAT LOVE IS THIS?

In spite of many differences of opinion among Calvinists today, Calvinism is generally explained by the acronym, T.U.L.I.P. Philip F. Congdon writes that "a tulip is a beautiful flower, but bad theology.

"The fruit of the flower is appealing; the fruit of the theology is appalling... works, as an inevitable result, are necessary for salvation. To be fair, Classical Calvinists usually object to this by describing the gospel message as not 'faith + works = justification,' but 'faith = justification + works'.... This is no more than a word game. It is best seen in the old Calvinist saying: 'You are saved by faith alone, but the faith that saves you is never alone....'"

Some readers may have never heard of T.U.L.I.P. Others, though knowing that it has something to do with Calvinism, find it difficult to remember what each letter stands for:

"T" STANDS FOR TOTAL DEPRAVITY
"U" STANDS FOR UNCONDITIONAL ELECTION
"L" STANDS FOR LIMITED ATONEMENT
"I" STANDS FOR IRRESISTIBLE GRACE
"P" STANDS FOR PERSEVERANCE OF THE SAINTS

Quoting from the major Calvinistic creeds or confessions (including actual citations and context from the Canons of Dort and the Westminster Confession of Faith), Dave Hunt proceeds to dissect the "sacred" T.U.L.I.P. one petal at a time—exposing each of Calvin's five points to the light of Scripture as a workman "rightly dividing the word of truth."

PAPERBACK • 190 PAGES • THE BEREAN CALL (2012) • ISBN 978-1-928660-75-0

A CALVINIST'S HONEST DOUBTS: RESOLVED BY REASON AND GOD'S AMAZING GRACE

—by Dave Hunt

A COMPOSITE FICTIONAL ACCOUNT,
BASED ON PRESENT-DAY PERSONAL TRIALS
OF TRUE-TO-LIFE PEOPLE

As we got up to leave, a young woman who had sat through the entire discussion in silence asked if she could have a private moment of my time. We sat down again, and she began to tell a tale of grief. She was a pastor's wife. Their lives and ministry had been happy and fruitful until her husband and two close friends, also pastors, became interested in a new "truth." All three were aspiring "intellectuals." As a result of reading current Calvinist authors, they had been drawn to the writings of John Calvin, Jonathan Edwards, John Knox, and others. Their study, taking them all the way back to Augustine, eventually became almost an obsession. Then each of them began to preach this new "light" from their pulpits. After being warned several times to desist, they were removed from their pastorates. Eventually, her husband began to worry whether he was really one of the elect. The nagging questions grew into full-blown doubts about his salvation. Calvinism, which had once seemed so satisfying, now began to haunt him with uncertainty. Was he really one of the elect?

The above excerpt sets the scene for Dave Hunt's 112-page paperback, created out of a need for a non-intimidating, easy-to-read "introduction" to Calvinism. Based on years of actual accounts and conversations, this quick-reading paperback is derived from material in Dave's much larger scholarly work, *What Love Is This?* In *Honest Doubts*, readers will become familiar with the key issues in a unique format that reads like a real-life drama, because the characters are composites of actual individuals, and the circumstances are equally real.

Discover the heart of a Calvinist "seeker"—and the surprising result of his quest for truth in this fictionalized but true-to-life dialogue: *A Calvinist's Honest Doubts: Resolved by Reason and God's Amazing Grace*. This approachable, inexpensive paperback is enjoyable to read and great to give away.

PAPERBACK • 109 PAGES • THE BEREAN CALL (2005) • ISBN 1-928660-34-7

CALVIN'S DILEMMA:
GOD'S SOVEREIGNTY VS.
MAN'S FREE WILL

—by Dave Hunt

SELECTED MATERIAL FROM THE BESTSELLING
HARDCOVER, WHAT LOVE IS THIS?

ONE OFTEN HEARS Christians say, "God is in control; He's still on the throne." But what does that mean? Was God not in control when Satan rebelled and when Adam and Eve disobeyed, but now He is? Does God's being in control mean that all rape, murder, war, famine, suffering, and evil is exactly what He planned and desires—as Palmer says, "— even the moving of a finger...the mistake of a typist..."?

God's absolute sovereignty does not require that everything man chooses to do—or not to do—was foreordained by God from eternity past. There is neither logical nor biblical reason why a sovereign God, by His own sovereign design, could not allow creatures made in His image the freedom of moral choice. Indeed, He must, if man is to be more than a cardboard puppet!

It is foolish to suggest that if man could reject Christ, that would put him in control of either his own destiny or of God. God is in control. It is He who makes the rules, sets the requirements for salvation, and determines the consequences of either acceptance or rejection. God is no less sovereign over those who reject Christ than He is over those who accept Him. He is the one who has determined the conditions of salvation and what will happen both to those who accept and to those who reject His offer.

But the Calvinist, because of his extreme view of sovereignty, can no more allow any man to say yes to Christ than he can allow him to say no. This error, having destroyed the foundation for a genuine salvation, creates a false one. And in order to support this false salvation that, allegedly, God *imposes* upon an elect, Calvinism has had to invent its five points. This fact will become ever more clear in *Calvin's Dilemma*. (SLATED FOR RELEASE IN 2013)

PAPERBACK • THE BEREAN CALL (2013) • ISBN 978-1-928660-78-1

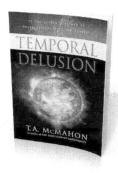

TEMPORAL DELUSION:
IS THE CHURCH DESTINED TO BE RAPTURED—OR TO REIGN SUPREME? —*by T. A. McMahon*

"These all died in faith, not having received the promises, but having seen them afar off, and were persuaded of them, and embraced them, and confessed that they were strangers and pilgrims on the earth. For they...declare plainly that they seek a country....
But now they desire a better country, that is, an heavenly...." —HEBREWS 11:13-16

AT THIS VERY MOMENT, millions of professing Christians are joining with millions of other "believers" to promote peace and reconciliation across the country and around the globe. These pragmatic, purpose-driven churches and organizations are uniting for the ecumenical "common good" to eliminate poverty, eradicate disease, and save the earth from political and environmental disaster—all in the name of advancing "God's kingdom on earth." But are all of these good works derived from a biblical blueprint for humanity? Or are these well-meaning workers building a house on foundations of sand?

Furthermore, is the great commission of the church being compromised by ignoring the clear and unmistakable roadmap in Scripture concerning End Times events, including Christ's "catching up" of the saints? Does it really matter what one believes about the Rapture in these increasingly perilous times?

If you seek to understand current church trends in the light of God's revealed and perfect Word, you'll find this easy-to-read volume both helpful and heart-pricking concerning the true state of the church today. In the process, you'll discover that what you believe about "controversial" Last Days doctrines should indeed impact the direction and focus of our daily Christian walk—encouraging and equipping us to set about "redeeming the time, for the days are evil" (Ephesians 5:16).

PAPERBACK • 157 PAGES • THE BEREAN CALL (2011) • ISBN 978-1-928660-71-2

ABOUT THE BEREAN CALL

The Berean Call (TBC) is a non-denominational, tax-exempt organization which exists to:

ALERT believers in Christ to unbiblical teachings and practices impacting the church

EXHORT believers to give greater heed to biblical discernment and truth regarding teachings and practices being currently promoted in the church

SUPPLY believers with teaching, information, and materials which will encourage the love of God's truth, and assist in the development of biblical discernment

MOBILIZE believers in Christ to action in obedience to the scriptural command to "earnestly contend for the faith" (Jude 3)

IMPACT the church of Jesus Christ with the necessity for trusting the Scriptures as the only rule for faith, practice, and a life pleasing to God

A free monthly newsletter, THE BEREAN CALL, may be received by sending a request to: PO Box 7019, Bend, OR 97708; or by calling

1-800-937-6638

To register for free email updates, to access our digital archives, and to order a variety of additional resource materials online, visit us at:

www.thebereancall.org